Just When I Thought
I'd Dropped My Last Egg

Just When
I Thought I'd Dropped
My Last Egg

LIFE and OTHER CALAMITIES

Kathie Lee Gifford

BALLANTINE BOOKS / NEW YORK

Published in the United States by Ballantine Books,
an imprint of The Random House Publishing Group,
a division of Random House, Inc., New York.

BALLANTINE and colophon are registered trademarks
of Random House, Inc.

Grateful acknowledgment is made to CassyCody Music LTD / Upward Spiral
Entertainment / Sony/ATV Harmony (ASCAP) for permission to reprint the
song "He Is with You" from the stage musical *Under the Bridge*. Lyrics by
Kathie Lee Gifford. Music by David Pomeranz. © CassyCody Music LTD /
Upward Spiral Entertainment / Sony/ATV Harmony (ASCAP).

Grateful acknowledgment is made to the following photographers for
permission to reprint their work:
Photograph on page 20 copyright © 1996 by Steve Friedman
Photograph on page 89 copyright © by Dana Fineman
Photograph on page 99 copyright © by David O. Marlow
Photograph on page 103 copyright © 1998 by Sonia Moskowitz
Photograph on page 244 copyright © 1994 by Steve Friedman

Library of Congress Cataloging-in-Publication Data
Gifford, Kathie Lee.
Just when I thought I'd dropped my last egg: life and other calamities /
Kathie Lee Gifford.
p.   cm.
ISBN 978-0-345-51206-2
1. Gifford, Kathie Lee.   2. Television personalities—
United States—Biography.   I. Title
PN1992.4.G54A3 2009
791.45'028'092—dc22   2009002153
[B]

Printed in the United States of America on acid-free paper

www.ballantinebooks.com

2 4 6 8 9 7 5 3 1

First Edition

Book design by Susan Turner

Fifty-six years ago a beautiful woman named Joanie dropped an egg and named it me. She has been an inspiration, a comfort, a strength, and an exasperation because she has been a very good mother.

I dedicate these pages to her because, together with my daddy, she taught me how to live, how to grow, and how to dream.

But it was Joanie who taught me how to laugh.

I love you, Mom.

Thank you.

The cock crows, but the hen delivers the goods.

—Anon.

Introduction

I REMEMBER MY MOTHER POIGNANTLY SAYING TO ME MANY YEARS ago, "I'm an eighteen-year-old girl trapped in a fifty-three-year-old woman's body."

I had no idea what she meant at the time, but today, being a good two years older than she was then, I find myself nodding in sad recognition.

Thankfully, we live in a world where fifty is the new thirty, and many of us are way ahead of our mothers in understanding the benefits of good nutrition and exercise and the importance of being proactive regarding our own health.

And let's be honest, we also have many more options today than our mothers did when it comes to advances in plastic surgery and dermatology.

So we're living longer and looking better longer than ever. But we're also suffering from more heart disease, more cancer, more depression, and more stress than at any other time in history.

Are we happier than our mothers were? Are we any wiser? Are we more content with our lives as we get closer and closer to equality in a "man's world"?

I guess it depends on who you talk to.

I can only speak for myself.

So here goes . . .

I have lived a very weird life, and while I'm not ashamed of it, I am sometimes embarrassed by the painful publicness of it. I have traveled down strange paths and have made camp in lonely places. I have dined with the dying and had cocktails with kings. I have seen injustice and I have seen miracles. Both have moved me to tears and to action. I have lived in the spotlight and under the microscope. And I have cried for days in the Valley of Despair and yet awakened on the mountaintop of a beautiful thing called Mercy.

Sound familiar?

It's called LIFE, and I'm sure you can relate to a lot of it.

So I have written this book in a style that is representative of my journey. It meanders. It pauses. It turns corners, and it surprises. And one day it will end.

I talk this way on television and I talk this way at home. I'm slapstick-silly one moment and drop-dead serious the next. I find the humor in tragedy and the underlying sadness in laughter. And in all of it I find a glimmer of hope.

I hope you will, too.

Just When I Thought
I'd Dropped My Last Egg

Eggspectations

SINCE THE BEGINNING OF TIME THE SAME QUESTION HAS BEEN asked over and over again: What came first? The chicken or the egg? Well, I'm happy to say that I finally have the answer.

It's neither. The chicken's mother came first.

That's right. The mother dropped an egg and the first chicken was hatched.

And that's what we chicks have been doing ever since.

So, if you're reading this, I have obviously not dropped my last egg yet.

Oh, sure, I dropped my last *reproductive* egg a few years ago. But my fertility eggs? Fuhgidaboutit.

I'm Fertile Myrtle now. I'm back to a daily grind on the *Today* show after an eight-year hiatus from television, I'm producing my fourth musical for the theater, I'm in development for two screenplays to be made into films, I'm halfway through writing my first novel, and I'm under deadline to finish this book by Christmas.

In other words, forget about a pig in mud. I'm more like a pregnant pig in placenta!

I share none of this information in a bragging way—on the contrary, I am so overwhelmed with gratitude that I still find joy and wonder and inspiration and challenge each day that I want to encourage everybody else to understand that the same sense of creative fertility is possible for them.

For years our society has perpetrated the perverse notion that once nature is done with us—especially women—we're done, too! "ONLY THOSE WHO OVULATE ALLOWED!" But it's a lie, and we don't have to cooperate with it. Who says we have to hoist our beefy carcass onto the gurney and disappear into the sunset? Not me. Because you know when we're really done? When we drop dead, that's when. And even then it's a whole different discussion about where we go from there.

But until that day comes, I believe we can experience creativity far beyond our wildest expectations. We can give birth daily to something beautiful and meaningful in ways we've never dreamed. Because when we're older, we are free from raising young kids, building careers, and managing households, all the while battling Midol headaches. I don't bloat anymore! Now it's just fat, but that's another essay. Think how much money we're all saving because we bypass the feminine hygiene shelves at the drugstore. Okay, you argue, but what about all the hormone replacement stuff and edamame we need now?

You're right, nothing's perfect. But that's really my point. Our lives stopped being perfect the moment we slipped out of the womb and got our heinies smacked.

Right then we should have realized that those days of

sloshing around safe and sound in that amniotic fluid without a care in the world were over.

But, no. Then society started reinforcing that other ridiculous lie: that "happily ever after" crap.

We'd no sooner finish reading those fairy tale books when we'd start dreaming of our own Prince Charming, riding up on his Harley and carrying us away.

Oh, he rode up and carried us away all right. To a life of cooking, cleaning, birthing, and diapers. But we didn't mind, did we? We were doing what we were created to do AT THAT TIME in our lives.

But none of the books we were encouraged to read ever mentioned that Prince Charming might end up being a jerk or a lousy provider or even, unfortunately for some, gay, which is indeed problematic in a traditional marriage.

So even if he was a sweet, loving, hardworking heterosexual prince, chances are his breath stunk, or he was a slob, or he ate too much or developed hair in weird places or liked to play with his putter more than he liked to play with his wife. And if we women are really honest, we might even admit that we were no "picnic in the park" either. More like a "bologna sandwich in the backyard on a hot day with a storm coming."

Truth is, if you live long enough, you're bound to be disappointed and you're bound to disappoint others in return.

For me it's been a matter of coming to grips with reality. Sometimes life doesn't march on; it limps. Sometimes it's on a walker and sometimes it's on an IV drip in the ICU. What's for sure is that we're going to have ups and downs, good days and bad, triumphs and tragedies, shock and awe, and everything in between no matter what the fairy tales told us.

How we deal with it is ultimately what makes the difference between a life *well* lived and a life, well, . . . lived.

S'Age

I'M SO TIRED OF READING THE WORD "AGING." NOT BECAUSE IT'S A bad word in itself. A bottle of wine, a savings bond, certain cheeses, antiques, these are all examples where "aging" is considered an asset.

So why isn't that true of people? I mean, the opposite of aging is *not* aging. Therefore, if you're not aging—call me crazy, but I'm pretty sure you're dead. Now, I don't fear dying, but I don't particularly love the idea of being dead. It's just so final-sounding.

The problem I have is that the word "aging" is almost always attached to a celebrity of a "certain age."

Example: Madonna, the *aging* rock star; Clint Eastwood, the *aging* actor/director; John McCain, the *aging* presidential candidate; Kathie Lee, the *aging* . . . Well, no need to dwell on that. You get my drift.

What about Paris Hilton? Am I missing something or is she not aging at the exact same rate that all of the above are? So why isn't she referred to as "the aging celebutard"?

Scientifically, we're all aging one second at a time, day by day, year by year.

Thus the adjective is being used, really, to say something else. But, *what* exactly? That someone is beginning to *show* their age? Maybe, but that's not true of Madonna. She's fifty but she's got the body of a twenty-year-old. Granted, Clint Eastwood looks like the Rock of Gibraltar, but I think the Rock of Gibraltar is beautiful. John McCain? I think after five and a half years in a Vietnamese prison camp and cancer, he looks amazing. And Kathie Lee? She doesn't look a day under sixty.

Hey, it's not complicated. Every day has twenty-four hours in it. The richest person in the world gets the same allotment that the poorest person gets. The difference is the poor guy is better off. He'll never have to read "Bill Gates, the *aging* billionaire . . ."

Lucky schmuck.

Da Agony of da Feet

IF YOUR EYES ARE THE WINDOW OF YOUR SOUL, WHAT THE HECK are your feet? It's frightening to think what my feet say about me. If genetics are the "sole" determinator then my feet say that I am a hard-loving, hardworking (by hooker standards), much traveled, extremely gnarly person.

Oh, and one more thing, each of my big toes lives in a different zip code from the rest of my foot, so I bet that suggests a sort of schizophrenic existentialism. I don't have a clue what that actually means but it felt good writing it.

Anyway, back to my feet. Because they *are* fascinating. I remember my mother telling me about her grandmother and the horrendous pain she suffered from the crippling arthritis she had in her feet. My mother can be incredibly descriptive when she wants to be, and the picture she drew of Great-Grandma Florence Kathryn's feet succeeded in making me pray that I would never live to be that old. But I have. My mother's mother died of tuberculosis when my mother was only two years old, so Mom never did get a good look at her own mother's feet. But I have a sneaking suspicion they looked a lot like my mother's.

Now, my mother, Joanie, is a gorgeous woman from her ankles up—I mean, Miss America beautiful—but her feet wouldn't win an honorable mention in the Most Beautiful Pig competition at the county fair. They have more than their fair share of bunions (the size of Delaware and Rhode Island), corns, calluses, neuromas, hammertoes, and various and sundry other ailments. And just like our great-grandmother before us, my sister, Michie, and I inherited the feet from hell. We really shouldn't call them feet; they're more like hooves. Even in my baby pictures you can already see the beginning of a small growth beside my big toe. So it was inevitable that I would also someday have wicked-stepsister feet even if I did nothing but sit around on my lard butt all day wearing ortho-pedic shoes.

But noooo, I had to choose show business. Ta da! Two shows a night, on a raked (angled) stage, and grueling choreography—all in four-inch Manolo Blahnik heels. See? I was stupid long before Carrie Bradshaw was. Forty years stu-pider. I would show you these feet I've just described, but I'm not able to. Nope. 'Cause I don't have 'em anymore. At the age of fifty-four I took a good long look at my face. Then I took a good long look at my feet. And as much as I thought I could use a face-lift, it was no contest. Hands down, the feet won.

I was tired of my feet telling me where I was gonna go, what I was gonna do, and how long I was gonna be able to do it. So I made an appointment with a Zimbabwean surgeon (don't ask), and on November 16, 2007, I had both of my feet completely redone. I spent the next week in abject agony, and I spent the next month contemplating the murder of a certain Zimbabwean surgeon. Then, all of a sudden, miracle of miracles, the stitches came out, the pins came out, the ugly boots came off, and the Zimbabwean surgeon became a genius. I am now a veritable born-again, back to life Ginger Rogers. I'm seriously considering *Dancing with the Stars,* running the New York marathon, and becoming a Rockette, all the while moonlighting as a foot model for Manolo Blahnik himself.

So the moral of the story is: Reach for the stars, baby. But make sure your feet are up for the trip.

Now, about my face . . .

Cheers

Recently I was invited to a very chic, very sophisticated birthday party for my friend Barbara Taylor Bradford. Barbara is the celebrated author of twenty-four books and a fabulous woman. The magnificent private room at Le Cirque restaurant in New York City was filled with maybe thirty women of various ages, backgrounds, and interests. You would recognize most of them by name if I mentioned them, but I'm trying hard to keep from offending more people than absolutely necessary, so they shall remain nameless.

Anyway, after a delicious lunch it was time for the birthday toasts. The first to clink her glass and rise to speak was Edwina Churchill. With her elegant bearing and lovely English accent she began, "My grandfather Winston [yes, *that* Churchill] was a man of . . ." and she went on for quite some time about his accomplishments, which as you know from history were pretty remarkable by anyone's standards.

Finally, as Edwina came to a close, she lifted her champagne glass even higher into the air and said, "And so, my dear Barbara, my grandfather Winston Churchill would have *loved* you."

After we all said "Hear, hear" and took a sip, a deathly silence filled the once cheery room. I guarantee you the thought every one of us was thinking was "How the hell do you follow that?"

But being the fool that I am and always will be, I clinked my glass and stood to speak. (Hey, *somebody* had to!)

Looking lovingly at my friend, I said, "Barbara, my grandfather Meyer Epstein was a bootlegger, a snake charmer, and a carnival barker." I paused for dramatic effect. "And he would have loved you even more!"

Everyone laughed except Edwina, who has never spoken to me since.

What's the point of the story? I'm not sure, except to make note of the fact that our families are our families and each one of us has to come to some place of acceptance about that eventually. The sooner we do, the sooner we'll come to a place of peace about our own purpose in life.

Right, Edwina?

Cheers.

King Charles, the Omniscient

Most women go crazy over George Clooney.

Me, I'm in love with Charles Krauthammer. Oh, calm down. Frank knows all about it. Every time he turns on Fox News Channel, there Charles Krauthammer is, and Frank immediately says, "There's your boyfriend."

I make absolutely no attempt to persuade him differently. Why? you may ask. Why do I love Charles Krauthammer? Because he is the single smartest man on the planet, and knowledge is power. That's why.

So, if knowledge is power and Charles Krauthammer is the smartest man on earth, then Charles Krauthammer is the most powerful man on the planet. And we all know that power is the greatest aphrodisiac on earth.

P.S. I'm sure this is going to crush George Clooney, but he's just gonna have to get over it.

Mutt's Up?

THERE IS SUCH A HUGE DEBATE IN OUR COUNTRY OVER IMMIGRA-
tion. It's interesting to me on a deeper level than politics because we're all, in essence, immigrants of one kind or another.
Except for the Native Americans. Now, they really got the
shaft. Think about it. Only the ones that own casinos seem to
have gotten a piece of the American pie.

I'll admit, my ancestors didn't come over on the *Mayflower*.
I'm no pedigree. My dad's father, Meyer Epstein, came over on
a steamer from Saint Petersburg, Russia, right after the turn of
the century. That would be the century before this one—
around 1900.

He was a Russian Jew and he married my dad's mother,
Evelyn, who by all accounts was a full-blooded Native American. So we nicknamed Daddy "Sitting Shiva."

My mother Joanie's parents had completely different heritages. Her father was from a distinguished publishing family in Toronto, Canada, directly descended from the brilliant writer Rudyard Kipling. Her mother came from Brooklyn, born of German stock. Joanie's nickname was "Cuddles" Cuttell. Apparently Mom was very popular, but she won't tell me why.

So, Sitting Shiva and Cuddles fell in love as most human beings are wont to do, and they started a little dynasty of their own. Right off the bat they had David Paul, Kathryn Lee, and Michele Suzanne. Three little Epsteins, just like the Three Little Pigs, but more like three little Russian Jewish German French Canadian Indians.

In other words, "American."

Joanie, here with Dad, has that "Oh, you want *my* picture?" look down pat.

I KNOW Al Gore didn't invent the Internet. But I did invent Spanx. All right, not Spanx, exactly. But the concept of Spanx.

Years ago I wanted the look of a bare leg on TV but I wanted the control of my trusty Givenchy Body Smoothers around my lard ass, thighs, and stomach. So one day I took my scissors and cut my trusty Givenchy Body Smoothers right above the knee. Then I showed Regis on live TV. Then somebody saw it on live TV and invented Spanx.

Damn. SPANX FOR NOTHING.

Leaving *Live*

For eight years after leaving *Live with Regis and Kathie Lee* people asked me why I'd left. Like most huge decisions in one's life, there was no easy answer. The truth is that sometimes circumstances converge like one perfect emotional storm, and there, right in the middle of the tsunami, is the real answer.

In 1993 my daddy began to show little signs of forgetfulness and disorientation. First we thought it was just a natural result of aging. He was around seventy at the time, but as things got worse, we had him tested, hoping against hope that it wasn't Alzheimer's.

Well, the good news was that it wasn't Alzheimer's. The bad news was that it was something that in some ways was even worse.

Daddy had a disease called Lewy body dementia, a rare

but horrifyingly degenerative condition that lasts an average of seven years from the first symptoms until death.

None of us had ever heard of it before, but my sister, Michie, was on top of it from day one. I think she ended up knowing as much about Lewy body as Daddy's doctors at Johns Hopkins Hospital in Baltimore did.

Needless to say it was an emotional, devastating time for us, as it is for any family with a terminally ill loved one. I decided to keep the situation private. I never spoke of it on *Live* for two reasons: one, because it was just too painful, and two, because I couldn't bear to have cameras shoved into my daddy's face, trying to capture lucrative shots of "Kathie Lee's Dying Father" for the tabloids.

My daddy had lived his life with extraordinary dignity, and he deserved to die with that same dignity.

And so began the tremendously sad ordeal of watching him suffer as his once brilliant brain stopped sending the right signals to his various vital organs until they ultimately shut down, one by one.

My mom and Michie shared the huge burden of his daily care with so much love and devotion and tenderness that it would take a book to describe it faithfully.

My brother, Dave, a pastor in New York City, and I traveled to see them as often as we could. I shipped my daddy's beloved Maryland blue crabs to him even in the dead of winter, knowing that nothing delighted him more.

Until, of course, the day arrived when he grasped a crab and, unsure of what to do with it, attempted to eat it whole. I can't express the heartbreak of that moment.

From then on we all picked the crabs for him, especially my daughter, Cassidy, who loved feeding the small morsels of crabmeat to her Pop Pop bite by bite.

It was during this difficult time in my father's decline that I discovered a love for something I'd never realized I loved at all.

In the summer of 1999, while we were on vacation in Colorado, I got a call from my live performance agent, Kenny DiCamillo, inquiring whether I was interested in returning to the Rainbow and Stars nightclub for two weeks of performances before it was scheduled to close a few months later. I wasn't doing much nightclub work anymore, but the surprising truth was, I was interested. The room held special memories for me for lots of reasons, and I was sad that it was closing.

"Tell them yes, Kenny," I told him. "And I'll put together a whole new show."

Well, once I hung up the phone, I realized I'd have to acknowledge somewhere during the performance all that I'd been going through in the tabloids for several years by then.

And it wasn't pretty.

I had become the tabloid queen, which, by the way, is royalty you never want to be and a throne you never want to sit on.

In 1996 an activist named Charles Kernighan stood up in Congress and accused me of tolerating the abuse of underage garment workers in Honduras during the production of my clothing line for Wal-Mart.

It was like being hit by a Mack truck at warp speed. Frank and I were about a month away from opening Cassidy's Place in New York City—the new home for the Association to Benefit Children. The facility would help tackle the growing AIDS and crack-addiction epidemics among New York City's children by offering comprehensive family support services, foster care and adoption programs, integrated developmental day care for homeless children whose parents participated in employment programs, a mentoring program, and a therapeutic

day nursery for some of New York City's most medically fragile children, with a special focus on children up to age five who
suffer from severe disabilities and serious medical conditions
such as cancer and AIDS. This was a four-story state-of-the-art
facility on East Eighty-sixth Street that we had spent many
millions of dollars building—and much of the money had
come from the sale of my clothing line.

First Lady Hillary Clinton and I share something apparently extremely funny at the
opening of Cassidy's Place in New York City, June 1996.

Hillary Clinton, the first lady at the time, had agreed to
come to New York and cut the ribbon after several frustrating
years of construction, which had followed several frustrating
years of battling city hall. It should have been a joyous celebratory time. Instead it became a nightmare.

I had been an advocate for children since I was a child myself. "Surely," I thought, "no one could possibly believe that I
suddenly woke up one morning and said to myself, 'I think I'll

put a few suffering children to work today in some sweat-shops. Yeah, that sounds like fun.' "

Well, unfortunately, the media outcry was so huge and so one-sided that people did believe it. Or else they just wanted to believe it. All I know is that instead of opening a facility for AIDS and crack babies, I was suddenly forced to use all my en-ergies to salvage my reputation.

No one seemed to care about the truth. The truth wouldn't have sold many newspapers or magazines. And it certainly wouldn't have spiced up the nightly news telecasts.

So week after week Frank and I struggled to understand the origins of such a heinous accusation.

One day in the middle of the firestorm, I walked into the *Live* studio and said hello to our audience. One lady in partic-ular waved wildly to me, pointing to her dress, which I imme-diately recognized as one from my Wal-Mart collection.

"You look great!" I remarked.

Suddenly she turned very serious and said, "When that man said those things about you, I went right to Wal-Mart and bought *five* of your dresses!"

I was so grateful to her and to the hundreds of thousands of others she represented, who were supporting me rather than vilifying me.

I remember appearing on *Larry King Live* at the time, and when Larry said, "I guess the profits from your clothing line at Wal-Mart have really plummeted," I was able to honestly an-swer, "Actually, they've gone through the roof."

People had come to know me over the years through their television set, and nothing they *read* about me or *heard* about me changed what they *knew* about me: I wasn't perfect, but there was no way on God's green earth I would ever do any-thing to knowingly hurt a child.

I wanted to hug that lady, and after the show, I actually did.

People like this wonderful woman, along with my family and incredibly faithful friends, sustained me through the ugly months that followed. Unless you have stood before a press corps that is licking their chops in anticipation of your soon-to-be ripped-off flesh, it's impossible for you to fully understand what this experience was like.

I used to open my eyes in the morning after a fitful sleep, relieved to realize I had been having a nightmare, but as the world focused, it would sadly dawn on me that all the evil and ugliness was real. I would gird all the strength I had for the day and the battle ahead.

I'll tell you one thing. You sure learn who your real friends are. The ones who distanced themselves at the time are still distanced. And the ones who drew closer are nearer than they'll ever know.

"You shall know the truth, and the truth will set you free" are the truest words I know.

Even in the darkest days, I found a strange solace in the knowledge that I'd *had no knowledge* of any abuse of any kind.

What we eventually found out was that the man behind the media firestorm was a union organizer. The National Labor Committee he worked for had an office at the UNITE apparel union in New York City, and Charles Kernighan, my accuser, was presumably hoping that by dragging me into a national media frenzy, Wal-Mart would finally be forced to unionize because of the public shame. That didn't happen.

What did happen is that our family went through several years of absolute hell.

Yes, Cassidy's Place opened. Yes, Hillary Clinton cut the

ribbon. Yes, I continued on *Live with Regis and Kathie Lee.* But I would never be the same human being I'd been before.

I can't describe what it's like to have everything you stand for, everything you've worked for your whole life, held up for public ridicule and contempt by people who couldn't care less whether you deserve the ridicule or not.

It was the first time in my life when I actually contemplated taking my children and raising them in another country.

This wasn't the America I believed in. This wasn't the country my father had defended in World War II.

And this certainly wasn't the America I wanted to teach my children to love and support and respect. All I wanted to do was quit my clothing line and remove myself from any association with such obscenity. But President Clinton asked me to stay on. Labor Secretary Robert Reich asked me to stay. So did New York governor George Pataki and New York attorney general Dennis Vacco. Every one of them believed that my involvement in the political process would result in much needed reform.

So I prayed like a woman on death row.

Prayer has always been a way of life for me, but I held on to it for dear life then. I prayed for guidance and strength and courage—everything I didn't have at the time and needed so desperately.

Well, to make a long story even longer, I stayed, and I fought for legislative changes. I testified before Congress and I spent months working with President Clinton on his newly formed Fair Labor Committee.

We passed the Hot Goods Bill in Albany, New York, that had been languishing in committee for nine years. Nine days after I lobbied for it, it became law, assuring that any goods confiscated from a sweatshop could be sold and the money given to the laborers who had been abused in the sweatshop.

It was work for which I had no training, and work I had no desire to be involved with. But it was work that I sensed I had to do, because I believe that everything happens for a reason.

President Clinton convinced me that by staying in the arena, I could effect change that no one had been able to effect for a hundred years, since my grandfather Meyer Epstein had sailed to America during the industrial revolution.

If that was the case, then I could only hope to see some greater purpose for this horrible personal experience.

Then, a couple of months after the initial accusation in Congress, I met with Charles Kernighan and a young Honduran woman who claimed she had worked in one of "my" factories.

It didn't seem to matter to anyone that I didn't actually own any factories, and therefore had never hired any workers to sew my clothes. I had simply agreed to license my name to Wal-Mart, which then was responsible for the manufacturing of my line.

Regardless, we agreed to meet at Cardinal O'Connor's residence in New York City, across the street from Saint Patrick's Cathedral.

Now, I am not Catholic, but I had a profound respect for this man and I trusted him. So did Frank.

The meeting droned on. At one point I received a note asking me to stay and visit privately with the cardinal after the meeting concluded. Of course I agreed.

And it was there in a small room standing alone with him that my life changed.

I had been very stoic up until this point. I had reined in my emotions the best I could under the circumstances, but when I looked up into the kindest eyes I had seen in what seemed like years, I simply fell apart and clung to him, sobbing.

"Oh, Kathie," he said so tenderly. "Remember this. Our Lord did not change this world so much through His miracles as He did through his suffering."

I nodded that I understood. The cardinal smiled, and then he looked deep into my eyes.

"And if you are willing to suffer this injustice for His sake, imagine how He can use you to relieve the suffering of others."

His words pierced my heart and got my eyes off my biggest enemy—me.

Yes, it wasn't fair what I was going through. But my ordeal was nothing compared to the oppressive, chronic suffering of workers of all ages in very real sweatshops around the world. Suddenly I was ashamed of my own self-centeredness.

I left the cardinal's residence that day with a fire in my gut to do all I could do to alleviate the injustice, regardless of what the headlines said.

One month later, Charles Kernighan apologized to me and my family for any adversity we had experienced. Never read or heard that anywhere, did you?

It seemed like no one cared. But a year later, *everyone* cared when a tabloid gleefully reported my husband's infidelity and exploited it for profit for months.

Thus began our second consecutive year in tabloid hell. We survived it, thank God, and there's no reason to regurgitate it all over again here. If you've been to the grocery store, you know all about it.

Except that, once again, through the words of a very wise man, I came to a pivotal juncture in my life.

"Kathie," he said to me during one of our weekly counseling sessions, "if you can't forgive your husband, forgive your children's father."

That began our journey of healing that continues to this day. So this was the state I was in when I hung up the phone with my agent a few pages ago.

I knew I'd have to do a musical number addressing my years as the all-time bestselling tabloid queen of America. (This, of course, was long before Britney Spears usurped my throne.)

So I called two of my dear friends, David Zippel and David Friedman, for help. Both Davids are brilliant lyricists. David Zippel won the Tony for *City of Angels* and has written many successful shows with legends such as Cy Coleman and Andrew Lloyd Webber. David Friedman worked for years at Disney, writing and conducting the scores for various films and Broadway shows.

In other words, I called the best.

And independently they each told me the same thing: "I can't write it. I didn't *live* it."

David Friedman encouraged me to write down some thoughts on my own experiences. So I did just that, and an hour and a half later I faxed my efforts to him.

It wasn't twenty minutes before he called me back.

"Congratulations!" he announced.

"Why?" I asked.

"Because you've written your first song."

And before I could utter my response he said, "Want to hear it?"

Such is the genius of David Friedman. It had literally taken him all of twenty minutes to take my lyrics and set them to music—brilliantly.

"Sure!" I laughed. And that's when I heard him sing over the telephone my very first song, "You Sell." It's a very funny, self-deprecating satirical account of my trip to tabloid hell.

Well, it was the hit of my engagement at Rainbow and Stars and the beginning of a very prolific collaboration with David. We have written well over a hundred songs together, and just this past fall joined forces on the *Today* show to launch our Everyone Has a Story contest.

And this is where my story segues into yours. I didn't have any idea that I could write lyrics, or melodies or screenplays or the books to musicals.

In fact, if someone had told me ten years ago that my fourth musical, *Saving Aimee,* would be waiting for a Broadway theater to open up, I would have had them committed.

Because I had put myself in a box and labeled it "This is who I am and this is what I do."

Well, what if there's so much more we *could* do if only someone believed that we could do it? Or if we ourselves believed we could do it?

I've known forever that the person people saw on TV with Regis every morning for fifteen years was just a shadow of the real person I am. Because there was a limit to what I could do or express on national television during that time of the day.

But I could show a little more on a sitcom or in a movie or on Broadway, or by guest-hosting the *Late Show with David Letterman* or *Larry King Live,* for example.

Everybody is multidimensional. All you have to do is spend a little time with any person and you will learn their likes and dislikes, their hobbies, their passions, and their hidden talents. Very soon you will realize that they are much more than your initial impression of them. They will surprise you.

Within months of writing, "You Sell," I had written a hundred sets of lyrics to songs. Some of them are still in their original state—still waiting for someone to give them a melody and let them be sung.

Others have gone on to be recorded by other artists, or to find a permanent place in one of my musicals or CDs.

This "undiscovered till a ripe old age" passion has absolutely revolutionized my life. My family would actually say that it has become an obsession.

Well, if I'm obsessed, then hallelujah! Because I am at my absolute most alive when I am lost in a world of couplets, alliterations, and perfect rhymes.

My rhyming dictionary looks like it survived Chernobyl. And in a way I feel like I have, too.

An old Confucius proverb says, "Happy is the man who loves what he does so much he never has to work."

Or as that great old Jewish philosopher Sitting Shiva always said, "Find something you love to do and then figure out a way to get paid for it."

It was ultimately my daddy who changed the course of my life in ways I could never have foreseen.

By the end of 1999 he had deteriorated badly. By all medical reasoning, he was close to the end of the seven-year cycle of Lewy body dementia. He still knew us, thank God, but he was completely dependent on my mom and Michie for his every need.

On the very last day of *Live,* my kids gave me a box of pancake mix. It was their sarcastic little way of saying, "Okay, Mom, let's see if you can be a normal mother."

Well, nine years later it's still waiting in the cupboard. We've survived a lot as a family, and it ain't over yet. But I wouldn't have missed a minute of it for the world.

Women often try to have it all, and I think that's possible, but not all at the same time. Something's gotta give, and I never wanted it to be my children. They are the final reason I left *Live* to have a different kind of life. They had been in the spotlight since they'd been born, but the world had changed a great deal during their short lifetimes. Gone was the spotlight, which is something you can walk in and out of without too much neurosis. Instead, our lives had been put under a *microscope,* and a microscope burns everything that's under it for too long. It was time to pull back and redefine what our family could be.

When Cassidy was one, I got a very exciting phone call from Julie Andrews and her husband, Blake Edwards. They were about to begin an ambitious production of *Victor/Victoria* and wanted me to take over for Julie on Tuesday nights for the entire run on Broadway.

It was heady stuff for a girl from Bowie, Maryland, who had dreamed of Broadway since before she could say the word. But ultimately it wasn't a difficult decision at all. I remember saying to Julie, "I can't believe I'm saying no to Mary Poppins, but I have to. My daughter is only one year old, and we'll never have this year together again. Broadway can wait, but Cassidy can't."

Julie reacted exactly the way you would think she would. "Kathie," she told me in that charmingly proper British way of hers, "I had to make the same decisions when my children were young. You will never regret it when you put them first, but you'll always regret it when you don't."

She confirmed for me what I already knew in my heart. Seven years later, of course, Carol Burnett and Stephen Sondheim made me the same offer, different show, and this time the timing was perfect. I agreed to appear on Broadway on Tuesday nights in *Putting It Together* so Carol Burnett could have an extra day off. Let me tell you something. After thirty-seven years in show business, it did not get any better than performing on Broadway in a Stephen Sondheim musical. It was absolutely thrilling, my only regret being that my daddy couldn't be in the audience and enjoy every performance.

When *Putting It Together* closed in February 2000, I had something I had never had before: rave reviews.

I mean it. If I had been dependent on glowing reviews, my career would have lasted about an hour and a half. So nobody was more surprised or delighted than I was at the reaction my Broadway debut received.

But it almost didn't happen.

I was supposed to start on Tuesday, December 7. (Pearl Harbor Day. I could just envision the headline: "KATHIE LEE BOMBS ON BROADWAY.") But the Friday before my opening, I had my one and only technical rehearsal—that's when you finally get the chance to do the show with the cast, in wardrobe and makeup, with orchestra, lighting, and sound. There was a potential stagehand strike looming that could have shut down Broadway over the coming weekend. Everyone was nervous about it.

But I did the dress rehearsal and went back to my dressing room to wait for Stephen Sondheim, who was going to give me his notes on my performance. That thought alone has sent terror through many an actor's bones over the years, let me tell you.

A few minutes later, in walked Stephen. I held my breath and waited for his legendary, and often painful to hear, observations.

"Sing 'doot-i-ful' instead of 'duty-ful,' " he said.

"Okay," I answered. Surely there was more.

"Sing 'France' that rhymes with 'pants,' " he added.

"Okay."

That was it?

"Otherwise it's terrific. Just terrific."

I was stunned, but truly, truly thrilled. It was comparable to Shakespeare telling you, "You know, you're not a bad writer, kid."

As Stephen began to leave, I couldn't resist telling him something I'd been thinking for days.

"You know," I began, "even if the strike happens and I never get my Broadway debut, I want you to know that I have already gotten everything I could have ever hoped for from this experience."

He smiled a really nice smile and nodded.

"Because you did the work," he said simply.

"Yeah," I agreed. "I did the work."

And the work changed my life and the way I saw myself and the way I defined success.

Success is not what you get *after* the work. Success is what you get *from* the work.

And I was loving my work—the writing, the Broadway— in ways I hadn't since I was a young kid singing my brains out with Michie in a folk group called Pennsylvania Next Right. Sure, I loved Regis and I was grateful for all the wonderful years we had shared doing our show.

But this work—this was HARD work. It required discipline and devotion to detail and endless rewrites and gut-wrenching honesty.

And then right after the show closed, I was asked to be the first woman to guest-host the *Late Show with David Letterman*.

Again, without really thinking about the ramifications, I agreed to do it.

I had no idea what I was going to say or do. Was I ner-

December 7, 1999, my opening night on Broadway in *Putting It All Together*. Stephen Sondheim has never looked happier.

vous? A little. I've never considered myself a stand-up comic, but I'd been writing my own stage act for years, so I figured I'd write a few lines about my situation.

David Letterman was recuperating from open-heart surgery so I deadpanned something like "Who knew he had a heart?" and the audience ate it up.

The monologue portion went over really well, and afterward I belted out the song that the crowd had loved at Rainbow and Stars, hoping for the same reaction it had elicited before.

I took out "You Sell" from the mothballs and performed it to a surprisingly enthusiastic audience.

They put you on a game show and you la-la out a tune
It's swell, you sell!

They put you in commercials and you promise folks the moon
It's swell, you sell!
They put you next to Regis and you talk about your life
You fight so much together people think that you're his wife

You sell!
It's swell!

They put you on the cover, say you're cryin' the blues
It sells! It sells!
They say you're leaving Regis. That's supposed to be news?
It sells! It sells!

They put you on the cover, say your marriage is over!
They put you on the cover, say your husband's a rover!
They put you on the cover, say your kid is a brat!
You once were anorexic, but now you're getting fat!
They put you on the cover, say you're cryin' again
And the source, of course, is always a "close personal friend"
The next day you're battling with Rosie and pills
The next day you're going broke because of all the bills
But that's because of all the plastic surgery you've had
And now you're close to suicide because it turned out bad

How do I stay alive with all those cancer scares?
How do I keep on smiling when greeted by those stares?
How do I maintain dignity while facing all those lies?
How do I manage motherhood and keep those inner thighs?

ALL:
Who cares? Who cares?

There must be something missing from somebody's life
When they'd rather read about the plight of Frank Gifford's
   wife

Is this really what's become of what used to be news?
Perhaps the thing that's missing is a carnival cruise

But why are all the critics always picking on me?
Please tell! Please tell!
Why am I the butt of all those jokes on TV?
It's hell! It's hell!

Aw, I shouldn't take it so personally
To them I'm not a person but a personality
I sell! I sell!

The critics and the pundits ponder endlessly
When—Oh God, please, when—will we be rid of Kathie
    Lee?
I wish they had the answer, if they only had a clue
I would surely die of shock if I got a good review
But that's never going to happen; my future is secure
I'll keep filling pages that smell faintly of manure

BAND:
It smells! It smells!

They'll all be filled with drama, pain, misery, and vice
'Cause they can deal with any news except the kind that's
    nice!

At this point someone in the audience threw a bra onto the stage and it landed near the piano. I took one look at that bra and thought, "*Gold.*" I casually reached down, managed to put that 36D on, and continued singing the song.

You know in all sincerity
I treat it with hilarity
It helps me keep my sanity

Maintain my famous vanity
I've learned to laugh at rumors and to scoff at all the jests
Yes the press is tough and paparazzi are just pests
But you people have been great to me
You're the reason that I stay
With a lot of help from heaven
And a lot of chardonnay

BAND:
She drinks!

KATHIE:
Not all day!

They take your picture when you're simply scratchin' your eye
Then print "There She Goes Again Startin' to Cry"
When in fact you're really laughing 'cause you know it isn't
* true*
They're writing about someone, but that someone isn't you

If I believed the crap I read
How I'm a woman filled with greed
Who really is a heartless jerk
Who loves to put small kids to work
The hissy fits
The Gelman snits
The phony bitch with phony tits
Who slept her way up to the top
And talks and talks and just won't stop!

I'd hate me too!

Well, the crowd went ape. The minute we went to commercial break, something in my head said, "Take a mental picture. This is the moment your life changed."

The hour flew by as I interviewed Tom Arnold and Joy Behar, and the terrific Linda Eder sang, "Vienna."

After the show Frank and I joined friends for dinner and I told them then what I had already decided. "I'm leaving the show. It's time."

I called Regis first and told him. He understood. He'd seen it coming for months now.

"Look at you!" he had kidded me on the air. "All you do is write songs. . . . You'll write a song about anything. Why, you'd write a song about soup!"

"That's right," I laughed, doing my best Austin Powers imitation. "As long as it's hot and creamy, baby."

And so on February 29—leap year, 2000—I took a real leap of faith and announced to our television audience that I would be leaving our show at the end of my contract in July.

I had no doubts and I had no regrets.

Life was too full of pain—my daddy's illness. And too full of promise—writing.

I needed to make time for both. I was forty-seven years old and running out of dream days. Even though I wasn't exactly sure what those dreams were, I knew they were waiting and I knew they weren't going to come to me. I was going to have to go and get them. Daydreams and dream days are very different.

In my heart I remembered my daddy tape-recording me at the age of five, singing a little song a cappella into his ancient, dilapidated tape recorder.

"Mary had a little lamb, little la—"

Suddenly I stopped and asked him, "Where's da moosic, Daddy?"

To this day I can hear his tender, loving voice. "Oh, sweetheart, you've got to learn to make your own music."

I am, Daddy.

I am.

P.S. My daddy died on November 19, 2002. As my mom sat beside his emaciated body, she quoted the Twenty-third Psalm over and over again. At one point she recited for the countless time, "Yea, though I walk through the valley of the shadow of death, I will fear no evil: for thou art with me; thy rod and thy staff they comfort me . . ."

And at that, my precious daddy lifted up, took a deep, deep breath, and passed from this life into the next.

He lived two years longer than most patients with Lewy body dementia. He even lived eight days after all life preserving efforts were stopped. His brain had shut down all his vital organs, except for one—his heart.

You see, the heart has a mind of its own.

Get a Load a Hoda!

EVERY MORNING AS I COME THROUGH THE DOOR OF THE MAKEUP and hair room at *Today* I sing the same song to the tune of "Oklahoma!" which happens to be the state where Hoda was born. "Ho—da woman when the wind comes whippin' round the plain."

I do a different variation every day and it starts the day off with a laugh. Now I've added snappy choreography as well.

I love my new co-host, Hoda Kotb. She is an absolute doll and so much fun to work with.

I wouldn't be on the *Today* show if she hadn't ambushed me one day at Michael's restaurant in New York and begged me to host the ten o'clock hour with her. I agreed, and the rest, as they say, is old news.

But before I agreed, I asked her to have lunch with me.

You can judge everything about a person by having lunch with them:

Do they show up on time?
Do they have good table manners?
Do they eat weird stuff?
Do they laugh at your jokes?
Do they cry when you sing them an entire song?
Are they embarrassed to be seen with you?
And, most important, do they drink alcohol?

Hoda and I went to the Rainbow Room for our lunch at about one P.M. By five P.M. the staff was kicking us out to get ready for the dinner crowd. I had chardonnay; she had champagne. We picked at our food but did not pick our noses. And we laughed our butts off. But we also cried.

I didn't know that Hoda had recently been diagnosed with breast cancer and had subsequently decided to have a mastectomy on her left breast.

At that time she was in the process of going through reconstructive surgery, and she was incredibly upbeat and brave about it.

"So are you finished, then?" I asked.

"No," she answered. "I'm waiting for a nipple."

I looked at her. She seemed amazingly calm and matter-of-fact. I was so impressed. What a woman!

As we hugged goodbye in the ladies' room, I knew I would love spending time with her anywhere—but I just couldn't imagine reentering that morning show world again after such a long absence. But one thing was certain—I couldn't return to TV without bringing my newfound passion for theater with me.

So, after several months of quid pro quo, back and forth, ping-pong, deal or no deal negotiations, my contract was done.

I couldn't wait to call Hoda and tell her.

And I was thrilled that she was thrilled.

"But," I told her, "I'm sorry, I'm not working with you unless you have a nipple."

She started to laugh, thank God.

"I mean it, Hoda Woman. My contract specifically states that I will only work with people with nipples—no nippleless co-hosts."

Well, from there we both just wet our Spanx laughing. And that's when I knew without a doubt that I'd hit gold—again.

P.S. I still love you, Reege.

From our very first *Today* show, it was clear this was not going to be boring. . . .

Be Still My Heart
(Actually, No, Keep Beating
or I'll Surely Die)

I AM ONE OF THOSE PEOPLE WHO SAY YES AND THEN KICK THEM-
selves when they have to actually do what they said yes to. But
being the neurotically guilt-ridden person I become if I ever let
anyone down, I always show up. Silently muttering to myself
what an idiot I was for saying yes in the first place.

Sound familiar? Ah, you're a people pleaser, too. Well, I
guess it beats being a bitch, right?

And sometimes—in fact, quite often—it actually ends up
better than you could have dreamed. Such was the case a few
years ago when I agreed to attend a fund-raiser near my home
for the Westport Country Playhouse, a legendary and historic
but badly dilapidated regional Connecticut theater. Joanne
Woodward was the artistic director at the time, so the event
took on a bit more cachet because of her involvement.

Well, the Sunday evening of the fund-raiser arrived and I

found myself wishing I could snuggle up in my ratty sweat-pants and forget about it. But since I am incapable of forgetting about anything, I gussied up and went, *without* Frank. Because, unlike me, Frank is extremely good at saying no and promptly forgetting about it.

The event was held in a beautiful home, and it was already crowded when I got there. I scanned the room and realized I knew no one, and I almost called Frank to come and rescue me. But knowing he'd be watching a football game and would be pretty cranky about it, I thought better. Suddenly I heard a bit of a commotion and looked over to investigate. There, in the middle of a crowd of admirers, was Paul Newman.

I was tempted to join the crowd, but then decided that Paul Newman didn't need any more admiration and probably just wanted to get a drink, which is exactly what I decided I wanted to do, too. So I wandered off to the next room in search of someone I knew and a glass of wine to go with it. About half an hour later I suddenly felt a gentle tapping on my back. I turned . . . and there he was. Paul Newman. In the flesh.

Before I could say a word (which is *really, really* fast) Paul got down on one knee, took my right hand gently in both of his, raised it to his mouth, and tenderly kissed it. Then—then! He mischievously looked up at me with those UNBELIEV-ABLE blue eyes and smiled.

"Okay," I sighed. "Now I can die."

Paul chuckled and rose to his feet, and I hugged him. (Yes, I hugged him. And you know what? I liked it, okay? Sue me.)

"Paul," I said, "it's so good to see you. How are you?" Paul smiled that Paul smile, shrugged his shoulders a bit, and simply replied, "I have a pulse."

We both laughed, and he continued, "At eighty years old, that's good."

It was a casual, friendly exchange, and yet it spoke volumes about this man I have so long admired. My favorite people in this world are the ones who use their blessings to bless others. People always ask me, "Who was your favorite interview?" And I always answer "Audrey Hepburn and Paul Newman."

Because not only am I a huge fan of their life's work, I'm an incredible admirer of their *lives*. So here was Paul Newman, eighty years old, still able to make a woman's heart race, and still using his considerable talents and goodwill to make the world—even an old worn-out theater—a better place.

That night as I was falling asleep I couldn't help but smile. Not because Paul Newman had gotten down on one knee and kissed my hand, but because Paul Newman had made me realize that I have a pulse, too.

And, therefore, a purpose.

P.S. The Westport Country Playhouse in Westport, Connecticut, was fully restored in 2006, and if you happen to visit it, please take a moment to pause in the Gifford Family Garden and take your pulse.

P.P.S. That Paul Newman was some fund-raiser.

Sadly, shortly after I wrote this essay, Paul Newman passed away after a long battle with lung cancer. I don't think there's a person alive who didn't respect Paul Newman and all he did with his time and his talents and his energy to make this world better than the way he found it.

On September 26, 2008, they dimmed the lights on Broadway in honor of his memory. But nothing can dim this special memory I have of him.

Feud for Thought

A FAMILY FEUD IS USUALLY SOMETHING YOU LIKE TO KEEP PRIVATE, but playing Family Feud is a different animal altogether.

When Al Roker was hired to host *Celebrity Family Feud,* I knew it was just a matter of time before NBC asked the Giffords to compete. I mean, after all, we're family, right?

Well, I guess Matt, Meredith, Ann, and Natalie all said "absolutely not," because suddenly we found ourselves in Hollywood on the set of *Celebrity Family Feud.*

Only then did we find out that the three other competing families were Vincent Pastore's (from *The Sopranos*—yeah, that kind of "family"), Dog Chapman the bounty hunter's, and Hugh Hefner's Girls Next Door.

In other words, a freakin' freak show!

I think it was the first time in my life that I actually felt normal.

The kids, Frank, his granddaughter Christiana, and I were the last team to compete. They had told us to dress in "cocktail attire." Apparently we were the only family to get the memo. I still have nightmares about Dog Chapman's wife, Beth—with her platinum hair, tattoos, six-inch nails, and full leather regalia studded with large pieces of rocks. Hey, maybe that's what she wears during cocktails. Molotov cocktails, I bet.

Me, I wore a three-year-old Roberto Cavalli dress 'cause I'm a simple girl at heart. Cassidy and I had made a mad dash to Saks Fifth Avenue the day before and had found a glorious yellow chiffon summer breeze of a dress for her. She looked like a vision, in borrowed heels from yours truly.

Cody actually looked quite groomed for an eighteen-year-old, and Frank looked . . . well, Frank looked like Frank Gifford. Frank always looks like Frank Gifford. He can't help it.

Christiana had dyed her hair jet-black and, according to Frank, looked way too sophisticated and sexy.

The contrast between the Chapmans and the Giffords was immediately apparent: None of us had mullets, and I'm pretty sure every one of them did. Both families, however, had a sort of sick psychotic competitive spirit. We could smell blood.

We lined up opposite the rival team, nose to nose, and pretty much tried to intimidate one another by growling.

I think Dog actually barked, but I'm not sure.

Anyway, I started feeling feisty so I began to mock kickbox Dog, the operative word here being "mock."

Suddenly I hear Dog say, "Get her, Beth."

Instantly the leather lunatic got me in a headlock, cracking my neck. Yes, my neck. The one that had sent me into six months of physical therapy because of a severe herniated disc a year before.

I think I went through the entire game with my head tilted

at a very strange angle. But the pain gave me the incentive I needed. Now I wanted to kick their collective canine butts and send them howling back to the kennel they'd come from. (I say this in Christian love, of course.)

Anyway, we started the game. The team leader who hit the buzzer first got the chance to play and put points on the scoreboard. This is where Dog had a huge advantage over me: He makes his living cracking heads, and I make my living cracking jokes. He hit the buzzer like it was a three-hundred-pound escaped murderer, and I just stood there wondering, "What the hell just happened?"

Well, what happened is my family wanted to kill me. The Chapmans got all the answers right, and I could only imagine the humiliation we were all going to feel when we crawled back home. Then somehow the Chapmans missed an answer and we finally got the chance to play.

Frank got the next try at the buzzer opposite Beth. Unfortunately, he couldn't hear Al's question very well and hit the buzzer before the question was out.

Frank looked at Al. Al looked at Frank. Beth looked at Frank with a very satisfied smile. I wanted to hurt her, but I knew that was physically impossible. It became very uncomfortable indeed. The audience held its breath as they, along with us, tried to figure out Frank's strategy.

Trouble is, that *was* his strategy. Hey, it must have worked in football. He *is* in the Pro Football Hall of Fame.

The annoying buzzer went off that signified he'd waited too long, and Frank returned to the team a discouraged man. Cody cheered him up the way Frank used to cheer Cody up, and that made me tear up. But this was no time for a maternal walk down memory lane.

Because, as you can imagine, the Chapmans took this opportunity and ran with it. They piled up more points but then finally got three strikes against them and it was our turn.

Cody whacked the buzzer. He got it first!

"Name something that women stuff." Al said to him, a little suggestively, if you ask me.

"Their bras," Cody immediately answered. Now that I think about it, he answered this way too fast. (I decided to ask him how he knew this at some later time, when I could smack him without an audience seeing it.)

We were back in the game.

I don't remember what happened next. I only know that somehow a miracle took place and it was suddenly down to Cassidy. She was our last hope, and there she stood: a Ralph Lauren commercial nose to nose with a mullet-haired, tattooed, body-pierced kung fu expert with a very bad attitude and questionable hygiene.

Al Roker took a deep breath. "Okay," he said solemnly, "it's down to the wire. Here's the question."

I could feel sweat in crevices I didn't even know I had. Al paused dramatically. I wanted to hurt him, too, but Beth seemed to like him, so I thought better of it.

"With what animals do human beings communicate best?" he asked.

Suddenly Cassidy morphed into Wonder Woman. A very short Wonder Woman, yes, but Wonder Woman nonetheless.

Her hand went up and smacked down on that buzzer as if her life depended on it, because her life did depend on it. Cody would have done evil things to her if she hadn't hit that buzzer first. I, of course, would have been loving and forgiving—eventually.

But . . . she got it first!

I leapt six feet into the air. We all did. And then Cass looked at Al coolly and announced confidently, "Dogs."

DOGS! Oh, the irony of it!

We were delirious with joy. All over a stupid game! But we didn't care. We had won the first round!

The Chapmans congratulated us as graciously as bounty hunters can, and then it was time to play Vincent Pastore and his family, who had defeated those cultural icons the Girls Next Door earlier in the competition.

Can I tell you how happy I was that the Gangsters had already beaten the Bunnies? Otherwise we would have had to play the Girls, and there's no way that Cody would have been able to concentrate with that much cleavage staring at him.

As it was, nothing in life ever prepares you to play against "Big Pussy" and his loved ones.

You can't go to school for this kind of thing.

You can only forge ahead and hope and pray that God is not a fan of *The Sopranos*. Then again, you also hope and pray that if you win, the Sopranos don't whack you.

But we won again! Then Cody and I did the lightning round and the Giffords took home fifty thousand dollars for the charitable foundations Cody House and Cassidy's Place in New York City.

Let me tell you, we rode back to that hotel as if we'd just won on *American Idol*.

Ah. Victory is a sweet thing.

Best served up "Family" style.

P.S. What's that word again for a female dog?

P.P.S. I've been having a little fun here with the Chapman family. Truth is, they were absolutely delightful. *Especially* Beth.

WHEN I TURNED FIFTY, Frank teased me that he was going to turn me in for two twenty-five-year-olds. I laughed. When Frank turned seventy-five, I teased him that I was going to turn him in for three twenty-five-year-olds. He laughed.

I am now fifty-five and Frank is seventy-eight. And you know what? We're too damn tired to turn in anything and we don't think it's funny anymore.

Not one bit.

Frax-elent

I'M FRESHLY FRAXELED. THAT'S RIGHT, YOU HEARD ME. I AM freshly Fraxeled, which means I recently endured yet another laser procedure called Fraxel.

Dr. Patricia Wexler, my dermatologist since the dinosaur age, tells me that I am her worst patient: I am allergic to collagen, Restalyne, Juvéderm, and all the other stuff most people inject into their faces. And apparently I have the pain tolerance of a small rodent known as a "wimp." I also have a well-documented fear of botched plastic surgery.

Which means she's left with very few weapons in her arsenal in this War on Wrinkles when it comes to me. Thank goodness BOTOX discriminates against no one. And a little benign filler called CosmoDerm helps, too.

"Do as little as possible as often as you possibly can," she has advised me through the years. "And stay out of the sun."

Well, unfortunately, most of my sun damage came forty years ago when I thought that baby oil and an aluminum reflector would make me beautiful. No one ever told me it would actually make me look like the lizard lady with the shoe polish on her face from *There's Something About Mary*.

So Pat suggested I try Fraxel, a procedure she described as minimally invasive and quite tolerable if you numb for an hour before.

I guess "quite tolerable" means different things to different people. I bet it does to Beth Chapman.

Anyway, Pat numbed me. She gave me a Percocet. And an hour later, she Fraxeled me.

Honestly, it felt like someone was taking a razor blade and scraping it across my face while dragging a couple of layers of dead epidermis. But I tried to stay calm, not scream, control my bladder, and remind myself "This, too, shall pass." Sorta like childbirth.

And in fifteen minutes, it did.

I looked in the mirror, and you could have fried an egg on my face, it was so red and hot.

"No makeup for twelve hours," Pat warned.

"Oh, darn," I responded." 'Cause I feel so sexy."

So then you wait three weeks and repeat the procedure for five sessions total.

Pat tells me that if I stay out of the sun, the procedure will be the equivalent of a very minor face-lift.

P.S. It better be.

P.P.S. Okay, it's working. But, unfortunately, the tightening of my face is starting to make the rest of me look older by comparison. I guess I'm gonna have to endure a full-body Fraxel eventually or just give it up and grow old "gratefully."

Hey, there's a novel idea.

Too Late Now

I HATE LATE.

Recently I've been thinking about people who are always late. I mean chronically, consistently, perpetually L-A-T-E.

Maybe it's because I've been on live TV and live onstage for so many years that I've got a built-in alarm clock that automatically tells me, "Get your butt in gear, girl, and *go!*"

But what I really think it comes down to is that people who are always late are actually people who think that their time is just more valuable than yours and everyone else's.

When I was a little girl, I used to love to go into Annapolis with my girlfriends on Saturdays for lunch and a little shopping; and yes, I admit, to check out the midshipmen who walked around town.

My daddy would drive us all in from our house and then

spend a few hours in his insurance office while we girls did our thing.

But, invariably, a certain girlfriend would always keep us waiting. None of us could go until she got there. This did not sit well with any of us, especially my navy-trained father, who found it completely unacceptable.

"Do her a favor," he said to me one Saturday morning as we waited yet again.

"What do you mean?" I asked.

"Leave her," he answered. "Leave her once, and you'll never have to leave her again."

He was right.

I USED TO HAVE good legs. Now I
have good legs from the knees down.
Pretty soon I'll have good ankles.
Thank God I fixed my feet.

Whatever Works

My daddy was a naval attaché to General Dwight Eisenhower at SHAPE headquarters in Paris, France, after the end of World War II.

My mom and dad often reminisced about "the Paris years" when we were little.

"That's where we really fell in love," my mom used to tell us, using her "dreamy" voice.

Well, it's certainly where they made me. I was born in the American Hospital in Neuilly, right outside of Paris, in 1953. We lived there for only a few months before Daddy was reassigned, so I didn't even have time to learn how to say "goo goo" in French before my parents, my older brother, David, and I left for the States.

Twenty months later in Patuxent River, Maryland, my baby sister, Michele, was born, and right after that Daddy was shipped off to Wiesbaden, Germany, for several years. So I didn't really live in America until I was five years old, and Daddy served the final years of his twenty-year commission based at the Pentagon in Washington, D.C.

When he finally retired from the navy in 1961, we settled into a brand-new Levitt community in Bowie, Maryland.

Daddy worked three jobs: He became a distributor for *The Washington Post,* he sold life insurance, and he played saxophone at night in a group called the 5 Moods. But it still wasn't enough, so Mom sold chicken eggs door to door. Today women sell their own eggs on eBay. My, how times have changed.

My parents were the greatest role models a child could ever have. They made family their first priority. They stayed together when times were tough. They taught their children to respect others and honor God. They kept music in the house at all times. They encouraged imagination and they taught us that working hard is the only way to work.

My daddy was what you would call a no-nonsense, frugal kind of guy. Just to watch him eat his beloved Chesapeake Bay crabs, you would discover that not one iota of crabmeat could be found after he was finished with it. And he enjoyed every morsel, often taking hours to finish any meal.

So he taught us to savor every moment, every bite, and every blessing as if it were our last, because someday it would be. That is not to say that the Epstein home was without its share of drama. No, indeedy.

My mom, Joanie, is a strong-willed, highly opinionated, high-octane-estrogen-fueled emotional woman, and it was not unusual for her to throw the occasional chicken at my father or the convenient glass of iced tea at my teenage brother if tensions were running high.

She always kept things interesting, and she still does. God bless Joanie. But beneath all the ebb and flow of everyday living, both of my parents taught us that very little in life is valuable unless it has been earned.

Today I read Proverbs 19:18, and it blew my mind: Discipline your children while there is hope. Otherwise you will ruin their lives.

Wow! This was written three thousand years ago, long before PCs, designer threads, and MTV ruled the world. But it seems that all successful parents somehow understand this principle innately. Most psychologists agree that once a child reaches the age of six their personalities are pretty much formed, and it becomes more and more difficult to impact their integrity as the years go on.

Discipline them while there is *hope*. Wow, again.

In 1961 we were the twenty-ninth family to move into the burgeoning development in Bowie called Belair. It was one huge construction site, and Daddy thought it was a wonderful opportunity to teach his children about the value of hard work.

Several times a week after dinner he'd lift us into the back of the rickety old station wagon and we'd drive around the half-built houses and collect all the empty bottles and cans we could find.

But that wasn't enough.

"Show respect for people," he'd say, insisting that we WASH THE BOTTLES before we turned them in for two cents a piece at the market. We grumbled, but we did it.

We also got up at 4:00 A.M. during the week, helping Daddy deliver *The Washington Post* on his newspaper delivery route. Yeah, that was fun. Well, I earned my first fifty dollars this way. But, more important, I learned a lesson that has influenced everything I have done ever since.

I started auditioning in Hollywood years later, and I remember him telling me, "Don't worry about getting the job, honey. Just be so good they won't be able to forget you for the next one."

And, as usual, he was right.

I moved to Los Angeles in 1975 to pursue my singing and acting careers. I wasn't very good at either one—I had way more guts than talent—but I also had an already deeply entrenched work ethic that was unusual for someone so young.

I went on hundreds of casting calls. I got many callbacks but never got the job. I got discouraged.

But with each new call I got newly excited, too.

"Maybe this is the one," I'd think, sitting in a room of a hundred other hopefuls. "Maybe this is the one."

Then one day I auditioned for a brand-new children's show. I stood before the writer and the director and the producers and read my lines and sang my song.

I felt good about it and left the audition thinking "Finally."

Until my agent called me once again with the news that someone else had been given the job.

I was close to giving up and going back home to become— what? I had no idea. Then I got a call to audition for a remake of a classic game show called *Name That Tune.*

I showed up at Ralph Edwards Productions on Highland Avenue in Hollywood prepared to sing three songs.

But when I got to the reception area, there was no one there. "This has to be some mistake," I thought, looking at all the empty chairs. "I must be in the wrong place."

"Miss Epstein?" I heard a voice say.

"Yes?" I turned to see the pretty receptionist holding open a door for me.

"Mr. Edwards will see you now."

"But where is everyone else?" I asked her.

"Oh, it's just you," she said, and smiled. "Please follow me."

I walked in and stood before the usual group of strangers who were about to pass judgment on me once again.

But one face was familiar. Then it hit me.

It was the writer from the children's show I had auditioned for some months before! He smiled at me, and I smiled back.

I sang three songs. Ralph Edwards walked over to me, hugged me, and said "Welcome to the family," and within a week I had learned two hundred songs and was the La-La Lady on *Name That Tune*.

It was the big break I had prayed for. But *how*?

Well, Gary Bloom, the writer for the children's show, had been hired to work for the new show, and when the time came to announce auditions for the singer, he said, "No, wait. I think I have just the right girl. She was too sophisticated for this kids' show I was doing, but I think she's perfect for this."

That was thirty-two years ago, and I have never been out of work since.

Hope, indeed.

P.S. Let the kids fight over the will when I'm dead and gone, but tough luck. I will die with that first fifty dollars I ever earned tucked into my Spanx and a satisfied smile on my freshly Fraxeled face.

Getting (High on) the Story

RIGHT NOW AS I WRITE THIS ESSAY I AM SITTING AT A RESTAURANT called Angus McIndoe and there is a guy two blocks down on Forty-second Street scaling the outside of *The New York Times* building. Everybody's buzzing about it. Now, in the past I would have just said a prayer for the guy and kept my lard butt in my chair.

But, noooo. Now I technically work for NBC News, so I feel kind of embarrassed to be sitting here drinking a lovely pinot noir while I really should be getting THE STORY. I tell my waitress to guard my wine—I'll be right back, and I dutifully head around the corner to check it out.

I look. I look again. I actually strain. It's not easy. The building is very high, and I have a very painful herniated disc. (See "Feud for Thought" essay in case you forgot.) I see helicopters. I see people looking up. What I don't see is the guy climbing the building. At my age, however, I'm happy I can still see the building.

I suddenly notice that I'm in a group of kids, with two lovely ladies trying to point out to them exactly where the guy is.

"He's taking a rest," one of the ladies explains to me. "He does that every six or seven stories."

"Oh," I say, impressed.

She pauses.

"Hey, aren't you Kathie Lee?"

"Yes, I am," I humbly reply. "I'm covering this for the *Today* show."

"Wow!" they all say.

"Yeah, wow!" I agree.

Then the lady informs me that I am standing on the corner with all the kids from the Broadway cast of *Mary Poppins,* who just happen to be there on their lunch break.

"No way!" I exclaim, and we spend the next ten minutes talking about the theater and Disney and how cool is Broadway? Then I realize I'm going to be late for my lunch date back at Angus McIndoe, and I start to cross the street.

"But what about the guy? He's about to reach the top of the building," they call to me.

"Oh, I'll watch it on the news," I answer.

I mean, I'm a professional, after all.

One Degree of Separation Anxiety

I𝐭'𝐬 become a joke in the hair and makeup room at the *Today* show that I have about one degree of separation from pretty much anyone on the planet.

Something will come up on the TV monitor, and I'll say, "Well, back in '62 I was . . ." and inevitably there's some weird linkage. Well, I'll take weird linkage any day over weird *leakage,* but that's another essay.

Anyway, it's well established among my colleagues that I have lived a long time, met an awful lot of interesting people, and found myself in way too many strange situations.

The other day we were all getting ready for the show when suddenly someone being interviewed mentioned the possibility that there were yet more victims of the Charles Manson family, long-buried somewhere at his ranch in the desert. Everyone looked at me and waited. At first I pretended I hadn't heard the TV.

"Well?" Hoda goaded.

I hesitated.

"Finally!" somebody laughed. "No degree of separation."

I cleared my throat. "Actually . . ."

"NO!" they all screamed. They couldn't believe I could somehow have a connection to Charles Manson.

I can't believe it myself. But I do.

Let me take you back in time. . . .

I'm not exactly sure what year it was, but it was definitely sometime in the late seventies.

Michie and I did a lot of gospel singing back then. One day I got a call from a wonderful man, Chaplain Ray, who had a very successful prison ministry. He told me that he and Pat Boone were going to tape a television special at the Men's Penal Colony in San Luis Obispo, California. He asked if Michie and I would want to join them and perform a few songs.

I checked with Mich, we checked our calendars, and I called Chaplain Ray and accepted his invitation.

Michie got there first. I was scheduled to fly in the next day. So I was anxious to hear how it was going. She took a long time calling to give me an update, and I began to worry.

Finally the phone rang. It was Mich.

"Okay, there's good news and bad news," she said.

"What's the good news?" I asked.

"I went through the worst thunderstorms you can possibly imagine. The plane almost crashed and I almost died."

"Wow." I said. "What's the *bad* news?"

Michie hesitated.

"The bad news is that I *lived* and now Tex Watson is my bodyguard."

"WHAT!" I screamed. "Tex Watson, the Texas kid who is actually the one who butchered every single victim in the Manson murders?"

I couldn't believe it.

"Yep."

I still couldn't believe it.

"Oh my God, Mich—are you all right?"

"Oh, yeah," she answered. "He's really nice."

"NICE? I am getting on the next plane out and I am coming to get you right now."

I hung up the phone and busted my butt getting to the airport, praying the whole way.

How could this have happened? I mean, Chaplain Ray had mentioned Pat Boone, whom some people find scary, but he had somehow neglected to mention that one of the worst mass murderers in the history of the world was going to be our *bodyguard*?

I mean, Tex Watson is no Kevin Costner. That's who I think of when the word "bodyguard" comes to mind.

Now I was losing my mind. But the worst was yet to come.

When my plane touched down in San Luis Obispo, it was 114 degrees Fahrenheit. Michie and I had been asked to wear clothes that were in no way provocative—heaven forbid we look enticing to any of the twenty-four hundred maximum-security inmates.

I met Mich at the hotel. She seemed okay and informed me that Tex Watson had been raised in a deeply devout home in Texas, but had gotten into all kinds of crazy drugs when he'd come to California to "find himself." Instead, he'd found Charles Manson and had found himself serving multiple life sentences for seven horrendous murders.

Apparently, in prison he'd also found God. As Mich and I

entered the security gate, I was praying that this part was at least partially true.

We were searched and were asked to leave everything we'd brought (purse, etc.) at the entrance. No lip gloss allowed. I cannot describe the suffocating heat, made worse by the polygamy-cult-style dresses Mich and I were wearing.

It turns out that meeting Tex Watson was the easiest part of the day. The worst came a few hours later when Chaplain Ray, Pat Boone, Tex Watson, and Michie and I were standing onstage for the finale.

The warden and his wife were sitting in the front row, and twenty-four hundred of the unhappiest men you can imagine were screaming "Sing 'Helter Skelter'!" in the bleachers. By now it had to have been close to 120 degrees inside the prison. Most of the inmates had taken off much of their clothing and were either fanning themselves or masturbating in front of us. I guess those dresses really turned them on. Who knew?

Anyway, it was almost over, when suddenly the unthinkable happened: THE POWER WENT OFF.

We were completely in the dark, and the only thing I *wasn't* afraid of was Tex Watson.

You sort of go into a weird Twilight Zone mode when something like this happens. I looked at the warden and suddenly realized how truly precarious the situation was. He was terrified. His wife was apoplectic. I actually squeezed Tex's hand for support! I looked at Michie, and she looked at me. We were both thinking the same thing. "I DON'T WANT TO DIE IN THIS DRESS!"

But for one hour that was a distinct possibility.

So, you ask, what did we do? Well, I'll tell you what we did.

We all stood there on the stage, hand in hand, soaked in fear and sweat, and sang "What a Friend We Have in Jesus."

That's exactly what we did.

It had never been my favorite hymn before, but it became my favorite hymn that very day, I promise.

Suddenly, as quick as the power went out, the power came back on.

The warden and his wife were rushed out of the auditorium, and so, somehow, were we. I can't remember what happened next, nor do I want to.

But I do recall that Tex wrote me several times afterward, asking me to speak for him when he came up for parole. I couldn't, I told him. He deserved to stay in prison for the rest of his life for the terrible suffering he'd caused.

He finally stopped asking, got married, had conjugal visits with his wife, and ended up fathering several children. He still works in the Chaplain ministry and by all accounts has been a model prisoner.

Pat Boone went on to enjoy a long and illustrious career.

Chaplain Ray continued his magical mystery tour through America's prisons.

Michie moved out of California.

And me?

I got out of gospel music.

It's just too dangerous.

P.S. They should change the name of the prison to the Men's Penile Colony.

Loony Tunes

I CAN REMEMBER AS IF IT WERE YESTERDAY THE TIME WHEN EVERY girl wished she looked like one of Charlie's Angels. Farrah, with the tousled hair and perfect teeth; Jaclyn, with the flawless face and willowy ballerina body; and Kate, with the athletic physique and gravelly voice. Okay, to be honest, as cute as Kate Jackson was, everyone really wanted to look like Farrah or Jaclyn. I'm sorry, but you know I'm right.

Anyway, all good things come to an end, and eventually one of the actresses decided to leave the show and move on with her career. Hollywood was all atwitter about who the new Angel would be.

I was home nursing the flu one day when my phone rang.

"Get into town immediately," Sam, my agent, insisted.

"Why?" I answered hoarsely, cool compress on my head.

"Because they want to see you for *Charlie's Angels*," Sam told me, "but you've got to be there in two hours."

Well, I knew it would take me that long to get my fever down, much less get my hair blown out like Farrah's. But Hollywood is all about opportunity, and when it knocks, you better look like a knockout or you'll be knocked out of the competition.

So I dutifully did my best with what God had given me and arrived at the casting agent's door. I walked in, and no sooner had my butt hit the chair than she took one hard look at me and announced, "Well, I'll tell you right now you're not right for *Charlie's Angels*." I was already sweating, but now I felt a distinct urge to throw up all over my 8 x 10 glossy.

"Why's that?" I managed to croak.

She didn't hesitate. "Because we're looking for a *pretty* girl," she replied, as matter-of-factly as anyone has ever answered me before or since.

As I tried to respond, she landed another well-aimed blow to my solar plexus.

"You know, drop-dead gorgeous like Farrah or Jaclyn."

The bile in my belly was rising, so I took that as my cue to rise as well and get what she obviously considered my sorry-looking ass back home to bed as soon as humanly possible.

The casting agent dismissed me by throwing my resume into the vast pile before her. Then, as I was halfway through the exit door, I suddenly stopped and leaned my head back into the room and said, "When you're casting a cartoon, let me know," kicked up my heels, and promptly left.

I will never forget the look on her face. But that is the precise moment I knew I was going to be just fine in show business. It kills some people, but it makes others very, *very* strong.

Years later, just after Cody was born, I left *Live* one Friday and was looking forward to a quiet weekend at home in Connecticut. That evening my assistant, Mickey, called to tell me that there was good news and bad news.

"What's the good news?" I asked her.

"The good news is that *TV Guide* is having a contest for people to vote on who's the most beautiful woman on TV, and you've been nominated.

"What?" I laughed. "Well, what's the *bad* news?"

"You're number forty-nine out of fifty."

She was cracking up now, and it pissed me off, but I had to agree that it was pretty funny. Suddenly a lightbulb went on.

"Mick," I said, "call Bobby in props and tell him to have an apple pie and an American flag ready for me for Host Chat on Monday."

"Why?" she asked nervously, because she knows me.

"Because I'm gonna have a little fun."

And that's exactly what I did. I held up the flag, the apple pie, and a big picture of Cody and beseeched the nation to vote for me because a vote for me was a vote for *motherhood* and *apple pie* and the *American way*.

The next day I shamelessly baked chocolate chip cookies for the audience, hoping they'd vote for me in return.

And by Wednesday it was pretty much out of control.

Regis watched, stupefied, as I entered the studio in the backseat of a convertible that Frank was driving. I held Cody in my arms and waved at the crowd.

They went nuts.

Suddenly I held up Cody for the cameras and displayed his diapered butt for all of America to see.

There, written in bold black Sharpie pen, were the words "Vote for My Mom 1-800-TVGUIDE."

Well, I beat Jaclyn Smith by fifteen thousand votes, and the editors at *TV Guide* were furious I had ruined their contest.

Me? I kept thinking of that day years before.

"When you're casting a cartoon, let me know."

Then I sent Jaclyn Smith two dozen roses with a note that said, "To the real Most Beautiful Woman on TV. Sorry. Love, Kathie Lee."

She forgave me.

I think.

WHY DID GOD MAKE FLIES,

and why, oh why, did he put hair on women's toes?

Why does God allow two eyebrows to merge, thus resulting in a unibrow? And how does a unibrow contribute to God's plan for living creatures in the garden of life?

I've searched the whole world. Even had it Googled. There is simply no answer to these questions.

The Way They Were

WHEN DID MY BREASTS BECOME FLOP BAGS? I DIDN'T FEEL IT happen. There was no seismic activity. No bells and whistles went off. The dogs did not begin to howl, nor did the Dow Jones Industrial plunge. But somewhere in time my boobs did. There wasn't even any warning. Just one day they were singing "It's a Beautiful Day," and the next day they were singing "Go Down, Moses."

I remember when it happened to my mother, but of course, you never think it's going to happen to you. Now my daughter, Cassidy, gives me the same "look."

WHAT ARE *THOSE* AND WHAT DO YOU INTEND TO *DO* ABOUT THEM?

When we were little, Mom would put on a mock English accent and say, "It's time to bathe the body beautiful." Michie and I used to love to sit on the side of the tub while she did.

We'd dangle our (increasingly gnarly) feet in the soothing hot water and talk about anything and everything going on in our lives.

Suddenly there wasn't any room for our feet because our mother's beautiful breasts had without warning become FLOP BAGS, and they took up the entire tub. It was time to get an industrial strength Olympic-size Jacuzzi, just to accommodate Joanie's morphing mammaries. To this day my mom loves what she calls her warm "bathie." Half the time I call her, I catch her in yet another warm bathie and having a little nappy to boot. She's already clean, but that doesn't matter. I'm beginning to understand it's about the ritual, the memories, and, of course, the mammaries and "The Way We Were" and the way *they* were and, unfortunately, the way they are right now. I wonder if that Zimbabwean surgeon docs flop bags.

P.S. I think it's only fair at this point to identify the "evil genius" Zimbabwean surgeon. He is Dr. Michael Clain, and he is not evil at all. But he is a genius.

I Don't Want!

Have you ever noticed a group of mature ladies dressed in purple and all wearing red hats?

They're hard to miss.

They're members of the Red Hat Society, and they are a hoot and a half.

You have to be fifty to join, but if you're forty, you can be a Red Hat Lady in training and wear pink. The premise is simple: Fun.

But below the surface of just the frivolity and silliness of it, there's a real sense of camaraderie and sisterhood.

These are women who have paid their dues in the boardroom, the bedroom, the kitchen, and the PTA.

These are women who have empty nests but full pocketbooks, and they are eager to party, let me tell ya. Now, I am not a joiner by nature, but if I were, I'd hang with those ladies in a minute.

Lately I've actually been hanging with them a lot because David Friedman and I wrote a couple of songs for a musical about them called *Hats!* Usually I write for my own projects, but this was a collaboration of many artists. I was honored to be in the company of Melissa Manchester, Pam Tillis, and the composers of *Dreamgirls* and *The Best Little Whorehouse in Texas,* to name a few.

The director asked me to write a song entitled, "I Don't Want." It was a pivotal song in the show because the main character, Mary Ann, laments the fact that she is about to turn fifty, and she ain't happy about it.

Well, it took me all of five minutes to write it, because I was fifty-three at the time and was *really* unhappy about it. David always told me to "write what you know," and this is surely what I know.

I DON'T WANT

Life so far has been good to me
I have very little regret
I've saved up for that "rainy day" coming
But I wasn't expecting to get wet yet.

So it comes as quite a shock to me
After being a great mother and wife
That I find myself somehow, here
On the other side of my life.

SPOKEN:
"I just thought it would take so much longer to get here, you know?"

I don't want to be somebody else
I just want to be a younger me
Have people confuse me with somebody else
Like, say, Angelina Jolie.
I don't want what I've never had
I just want what I had before
Firm breast, tight thighs, and unlined eyes
God knows I'm not asking for more

SPOKEN:
"All right, I am!"

I don't want to see my mother when I see my own face
Don't want to see new hairs in a brand-new place
Don't want cottage cheese except on my plate
And when I starve myself on cottage cheese, I want to lose
     weight!
And speaking of losing, I don't want to lose my mind
Don't care to lose my hearing, not too keen on going blind
I don't want bunions as big as my feet
Or varicose veins as long as my street
Or cataracts or liver spots or pain or hot flashes,
Stretch marks, insomnia, or sudden mustaches
Don't want to wake up in a river of sweat
I ain't a spring chicken, but this duck ain't dead yet!

SPOKEN:
"YOU WANT A LIST?"

I don't want to be aggravated, agitated, obligated, exasperated,
     underrated, manipulated, intimidated, deprecated,
     dominated, dilapidated, denigrated, CONSTIPATED
But once in a while, I admit, I wouldn't mind one little bit
     being MEDICATED or INTOXICATED.

SPOKEN:

"Truth be told, I wouldn't mind being stimulated and
penetrated, but hell, for that I'd need to be LUBRICATED!"

I don't need some damn doctor's diagnosis
I NEED A HUMP that don't come from osteoporosis!
I love life and I want to keep going
Without all the years of experience showing
I guess it's pretty easy to see
I don't want to be older
I just want to be
THE OLD ME.

I was really happy with the way it turned out but a little nervous about it passing the Joanie Test. So, after David added the music, we recorded a demo and I took it with me when I went to Maryland to visit.

"Now, it's a little bawdy, Mom," I warned her.

"You're always bawdy," she replied.

"Yeah, but this is even bawdier than usual," I insisted.

"Just play it and I'll let you know if it's too bawdy," she shot back, and so I did.

Well, she laughed so hard I was afraid she was going to have an accident of a certain moist nature.

"It's filthy!" she roared, drying the tears running down her face. "But it's SO TRUE!"

You gotta love that Joanie.

She has such good taste.

Chock Full of Nuts

THIS IS A VERY PAINFUL STORY TO TELL. BUT I HAVE CHECKED with my sister, and she insists that it is a story that must be told. She says it's important. Michie is very wise, so I'm going to go with her on this one.

Years ago Michie and I were scheduled to sing in Dallas. We were both in college in Tulsa, Oklahoma, at the time and our parents were visiting, so we decided they should join us on our road trip south.

We were generally new to the area so we weren't quite sure how long the trip would take. We asked around. Now, people from the wide open spaces tend to think a mere hundred miles is a skip and a jump, but we didn't know that at the time.

So we set out at around four P.M. hoping to beat the evening commuter traffic.

"How long could it take?" we thought. Two, maybe three hours? Depending on what happened with the weather and the interstate, we figured we'd get to Dallas in time for a nice dinner and an early start on a good night's sleep before our concert the next day.

For whatever reason, Mich and I hadn't eaten any lunch that day, but we'd agreed that a Texas sirloin steak would taste all the better because of it when we got where we were going. Well, guess what? We hit traffic, we had car trouble, and we finally arrived at our hotel late in the evening—like ten P.M. late in the evening, which is really late in Texas, unless you're a hooker.

All along we'd passed fast-food place after fast-food place, but we knew that hot baked potato with that sirloin steak would be waiting for us when we got there. Well, when we "got there," all the restaurants were closed. We called for room service. There wasn't any. They actually laughed when we asked. We looked for a mini bar. There wasn't a cracker. In fact, there was no stinking mint on the nightstand because there was no stinking nightstand. Nada, nothing, not a crumb.

Mom announced she'd had it and was going to go take a "warm bathie" and "bathe the body beautiful." Mich and I sat outside the bathroom on the queen-size bed and contemplated our fate. We were famished and forlorn, until suddenly we remembered, "THE BREAKFAST BAR!"

I had, indeed, packed one moist, delicious Carnation breakfast bar hours before. There was hope! We looked in my purse. No breakfast bar.

We looked in my suitcase, Michie's suitcase, Mom and Dad's suitcase. No breakfast bar.

We went out and checked to see if we'd left it in the car. Nope. No breakfast bar.

It was only when we walked back into the room that it suddenly dawned on both of us at the same time: MOM!

Instantly we raced for the bathroom door and flung it open, and there for the world to see was the alleged perpetrator in all her naked glory. The breakfast bar had indeed been eaten by our own mother, who, unlike her daughters, had had a big lunch just ten hours before.

How could we know for sure? By the chocolate crumbs floating on the bathwater, the smacking of our mother's chocolate-smeared lips, and the irrefutable evidence of large chocolate crumbs still stuck on her flop bags, that's how.

It was carnage there in that bathroom, and Mich and I were devastated that our own mother could have sacrificed her own children in such a way.

"I was hungry," was all she could say.

"So were *we*," we replied. "We still are."

"You're young. You'll live. You're always on diets anyway," was her final answer, and she smacked her lips like the vulture she was.

"In time you'll forget."

Not a chance, Mom. Not a chance.

P.S. Michie and I were both extremely pissed off about this and vowed that we would be much better mothers to our own children someday. And we have been.

P.P.S. We're still pissed thirty-six years later because we know that she would do it again in a heartbeat.

Fish Face

I'M ALL FOR PLASTIC SURGERY . . . IN THEORY. I JUST DON'T UNDER-stand why someone would spend so much money and go through so much pain to look like a completely different person. (Unless that person is Angelina Jolie—to look like her, I'd Fraxel every follicle I've got.) I mean, it's one thing to look better or refreshed. It's quite another to look like a freak. I am not going to name names. The point here is not to be cruel but to understand *why*.

What motivates an already beautiful person to undergo such trauma?

Eyes I understand.

Boobs I understand.

Stomach I understand.

Feet I really understand.

Pretty much anywhere on the body I understand if it drives you crazy every time you look at it.

EXCEPT THE LIPS.

Now, I love fish swimming in the sea or swimming in a lemon sauce, but flounders are not exactly attractive when they're attached to someone's face. And that's all I can think of when I see someone with enormous flippers—I mean lips.

Most of the people I see having one procedure after another are truly attractive people to begin with. Many of them are women who made their mark in the entertainment business based on their looks, and now that their looks are fading, to stay competitive they feel they have to recapture the youthful beauty they once had.

But no fifty-year-old can compete with a twenty-year-old. It's ludicrous to try. And exhausting. Not to mention expensive.

Maybe one good thing can come from this global monetary crisis we're in.

Maybe we'll all just grow older together. And fat. And— SURPRISE—even happy?

Nah.

Say "Cheese"

FEW PEOPLE ARE OLD ENOUGH TO REMEMBER THAT LONG BEFORE I started on the *Today* show, I was a special correspondent for *Good Morning America* and the substitute host for Joan Lunden. It was there at ABC that I met Frank, and all hell broke loose. Or all heaven, depending on the day you ask me.

Anyway, one of my very first assignments was almost my last. Our producer, Susan Winston, called me into her office one day.

"Kathie," she said, "I want you to run over to Bloomingdale's and pick up a couple of cute workout outfits."

"Why?" I asked, panicking immediately.

"Because you're leaving tomorrow for L.A. to interview Victoria Principal," she answered, not even looking up from her paperwork.

"Tomorrow?" I shrieked.

I was stunned. This was earth-shattering stuff. Victoria Principal was the Eva Longoria of her day. In a word: perfect. And I was in a word: NOT.

"But . . . but . . . ," I started.

"But nothing," Susan said, leaving little doubt about my employment should I say no.

"She has a new beauty and exercise book out called *The Body Principal* and you're going to do a three-part feature on her."

Somehow I found my way to Bloomingdale's, L.A., and Victoria's house, where we were scheduled to tape.

I wanted to throw up—give up show business and become what I was born to be: a librarian, or anything else that did not require workout clothes.

Finally I emerged from the bathroom and, determined to get this over with, joined Victoria, all pink and perky and PERFECT by the exercise mats.

She was even more beautiful in person, which I'm ashamed to admit was quite a disappointment.

She was very sweet, but she took one look at me and said, "Kathie, you have a beautiful body, but you love cheese, don't you?"

P.S. I gave up all dairy products for one month, hoping to ultimately look like Victoria Principal.

P.P.S. I gained three pounds.

That's Neither Hair nor There

WHILE I'M HAPPY TO BACK CERTAIN CAUSES, I'M OFTENTIMES uncomfortable backing candidates. But one day I found myself at an event in Montclair, New Jersey, for a friend of Frank's who was running for the Senate. People were milling about sipping cocktails, and all I could think of was the horrendous traffic we were going to hit on our way home to Connecticut.

Suddenly someone tapped me on the back.

I turned to say hello. And there it was: THE HAIR.

The woman said her name, and instinctively I took her hand, shook it, and uttered some vague pleasantry.

But I couldn't take my eyes off THE HAIR. It wasn't an unattractive hair. No, on the contrary. On the back of her head that hair would have fit in nicely. But it wasn't on the back of her head. It was on the front of her face. On her left cheek, specifically.

And it was black and it was long and it might as well have had a sign on it that said, "That's right, I'm a hair. I'm here and I'm proud."

"Surely," I thought, "this elegant, erudite, sophisticated woman is unaware of THE HAIR."

How long was the hair? Let's put it this way: If there had been two more just like it, she could've braided it.

So I gingerly, and as casually as I could, attempted to brush THE HAIR away. THE HAIR swung to the right. Then it swung back. This is the moment when I finally understood the awful truth: THE HAIR was attached. Yes, THE HAIR was attached to THE FACE. And it wasn't going to go anywhere without a fight.

Suddenly, eyes blazing, the woman responded to my touch.

"No—" she began, but I interrupted her.

"NOOOO, I was just . . . Someone must have kissed you," I quickly replied, attempting to brush away the phantom kiss.

She looked me dead in the eye, like a showdown at the O.K. Corral.

"That HAIR is attached. And I like it that way."

What could I say but, "Who wouldn't?"

P.S. "No good deed goes unpunished" is a cliché because it is so frickin' true.

Nothing Could Be Fine-a

I've always tried to teach my kids the correct words for things. I've taught them that a penis should be a penis, although personally I prefer "wing wang" or "schlong." Less threatening.

Nonetheless, I've tried. But it's funny—Cassidy hated the real words. HATED THEM.

"Don't say 'breasts,' Mommy; say 'boobies.' "

"Don't say 'vagina,' Mommy; say 'gina.' "

"Don't say 'penis,' Mommy; say 'wing wang.' "

So I've done the best I can, but I'm only one woman.

One day when Cass was five, she suddenly said, "I don't have a wing wang, right, Mommy? Cody has a wing wang."

"That's right, precious. Cody has a wing wang."

Pleased, Cass continued. "And Daddy has a wing wang, too. Right, Mommy?"

"That's right, honey."

"And I have a gina and you have a gina, right, Mommy?"

"That's right, my darling," I said, hugging her, hoping she wasn't going to mention the dogs. "You have a beautiful gina."

Suddenly Cassidy became very sad.

"But I don't have any grass on my gina."

It was one of the rare times when I did not know what to say. I think I finally said something lame like, "Give it time, baby. Before you know it, you'll need a lawn mower." But I can't really remember.

PHOTO: © DANA FINEMAN

Dueling divas.

Sex Scenes with Mom and the Kids

I LOVE MOVIES, BUT I CAN'T WATCH SEX SCENES WITH MY SON sitting next to me. Does that make me an old-fashioned prude?

Come to think of it, I can't watch sex scenes with my mother, either, who *is* an old-fashioned prude.

I realize there's starting to be a pattern here, but I'm not really sure what it means.

Maybe I can't believe Cody's old enough now to see mature movies, which would mean I'm really, really getting old. But how does that explain my mother, who's too old to remember sex?

Boy, life is complicated.

I think I'll go watch *Enchanted* with Cassidy for the umpteenth time. The little chipmunk doesn't have a wing wang.

Where Is He When We Need Him?

ALL RIGHT, SO I'M STILL STUCK ON THE LITTLE CHIPMUNK WITH-
out a wing wang. Maybe that's the reason behind the success of
all these kids' movies—the true genius of Walt Disney. Parents
like watching them with their children because we're absolutely confident that no wing wang or boobie is going to suddenly pop up and take everybody by surprise. No awkward
moments trying to explain to little Susie what that big hairy
man is doing to that damsel in distress who's suddenly buck
naked and having a seizure.

I hate it when that happens. But more and more a perfectly
entertaining movie seems to turn on a dime and morph into a
foreign language porno horror flick. Suddenly you're smothering your kid's head into the popcorn and stuffing Milk Duds
into their ears.

I know it's silly. I mean, I realize kids see and hear worse at home. But there's something about seeing it on a fifty-foot screen in HD and hearing it in Dolby sound that's upsetting.

Walt Disney would die.

Oh, yeah, he did.

Bummer.

Gifted

Cassidy has known since she was a young girl that she wants to be an actress. This terrifies Frank and thrills me. I understand Frank's fear, but he doesn't exactly understand my enthusiasm. See, he would prefer that Cassidy become a librarian, which would be totally fine with me if that was what Cassidy wanted. I'd drive her to the library three times a day if that would help her become the greatest librarian in the world. But it isn't what she wants.

Cody, at times, wanted to be a fireman, a football player, a cowboy, and an award-winning director. We have supported every one of those dreams, regardless of how outrageous they seemed at the time.

I believe with every ounce of what I am that God instills dreams inside of us long before we are born. Psalm 139:13–14 says: You made all the delicate, inner parts of my body and knit them together in my mother's womb. Thank you for making me so wonderfully complex!

When I asked my first-grade teacher if I could produce, direct, and star in a play, I obviously knew what I wanted to do. Nobody *taught* me that. I just *knew* it.

Why don't we encourage our children to follow the dream that was placed in them long before they could speak of such a thing as a "dream"?

This doesn't mean I'd encourage our kids to do porno films. I just want them to be in the *construction* business instead of the *destruction* business. I want them to use their God-instilled gifts to make the world a better place.

If only each individual would be encouraged to use their gifts to the maximum. Imagine billions of happy, fulfilled people. Hard, isn't it? Because parents are constantly telling their kids to go to the right school so they can get the right job, so they can get ahead in the world. Ahead of what? Ahead of whom?

Can we even imagine what would happen if we encouraged their natural gifts regardless of our prejudices? It boggles the mind to envision a world of contented, passionate individuals doing what they were actually created to do.

So I tell our kids to listen to that still, small voice inside them. Do what they can't wait to do. Cody is studying film, and Cassidy is studying how to act in them.

Neither one of them is going to become an accountant. I just pray that they get good enough at their chosen craft to be able to hire an accountant to take care of the money they're going to ultimately make doing what they love to do, instead of paying for a psychiatrist to tell them how their parents screwed them up.

Poetic License

JOANIE IS AN AVID READER. SHE OFTEN LOVED TO SHARE WHATEVER she was reading with Daddy. This could range from the profound to the absurd, but Daddy was always happy to have her share it with him. He adored her. One day she read a particularly moving poem and couldn't wait to read it to him.

When she finished, he said. "That was great, honey. Who wrote it?"

She looked back at the poem in her hand and pronounced, "I don't know. Somebody named Anon."

P.S. Admit it. You wish *you* had a mother that funny.

Examine This

I INSIST ON HAVING A WOMAN GYNECOLOGIST. NONNEGOTIABLE. I have a very cute male internist, but I have banned him from my breasts—sorry, Cass: boobies—and nether regions. I just don't think he needs to give me a rectal exam when my *female* gynecologist just gave me one. It's redundant, okay?

He can have all the fun he wants with my blood pressure or my cholesterol, but leave my GINA alone.

Speaking of GINAS—and who doesn't?—my sister, Michie, has a female gynecologist, too. Same one for years. Recently Michie went for her yearly exam and was spread-eagled, gnarly feet in the stirrups, halfway through the pap smear, when her doctor said, "You know, the nurse just told me that you're Kathie Lee Gifford's sister. You never told me."

Before Michie could respond, the doctor marveled, "Come to think of it, you and your sister do look EXACTLY ALIKE."

P.S. It's extremely important for you to get your yearly exam, no matter who your gina looks like!

Rocky Mountain "Hi!"

WHEN CASSIDY WAS ONE MONTH OLD, WE MOVED INTO A BEAUTIFUL mountaintop home eighty-six hundred feet up in the Colorado Rockies. I felt like Maria von Trapp and would often burst into song for no reason and without warning. The neighbors loved me. NOT.

But, boy, getting to that house required some serious D-Day maneuvers. First we had to fly into Denver; and then it was about a two and a half hour drive through Vail, Beaver Creek, and finally, Edwards, Colorado, where we'd take a very steep, winding mountain road straight up into the clouds for about ten minutes.

One time we were flying into Denver and were fairly close to landing when the co-pilot, a lovely woman, came out of the cockpit to say hello. At the time I was discreetly nursing Cassidy. The co-pilot took one look at me, came right up to my bosom, and cooed, "Oooh! Is that your baby?"

I couldn't resist.

"No, it's some kid from back in 14B who was wailing his diapers off," I said.

She didn't get it, but Frank thought it was hysterical.

Rockin' in the Rockies. Cassidy, age four, and Cody, age seven.

Through the years we tried to get to Colorado as often as possible, but it was difficult with two kids and a two-hour time zone difference.

The kids always threw up the first night we got there because of the altitude, but it was worth it. Way better view than my sister's GINA.

Anyway, one Christmas we decided to have a party and invite our friends over to celebrate. I hired a terrific piano player who happened to be quite large in his piano stool, if you know what I mean.

He was well into *The Sound of Music* songbook when suddenly our friend Elvia took me aside with a concerned look on her face.

"Kathie," she said, "Cassidy just told the piano player that he's had too many hot dogs."

I was stunned. I had always been maniacal about teaching my children to be kind and not hurt other people's feelings. I found Cassidy and immediately said, "Cassidy Erin Gifford, you go up to that man this instant and tell him you're sorry."

Head bowed, Cassidy did what I told her.

She found the man and said, "I sorry you had too many hot dogs."

P.S. I also taught the kids to tell the truth.

Oh, well.

Honorable Mention

WHEN YOU'RE ON A HIT TELEVISION SHOW, YOU TEND TO BE HON-
ored with a lot of awards you don't deserve.

Such was the case when I was given the American Cancer
Society's Mother of the Year Award in 1999. Anyway, my good
friends Claudia Cohen and Phyllis George were co-chairs of
the luncheon and wanted to surprise me with a special guest
speaker. I had no idea what they had in store for me when I arrived at the Waldorf-Astoria Hotel with Frank and my ingrate
children.

I walked into the ballroom, and there standing before me
was Kevin Costner. I suddenly found it hard to breathe or con-
struct a coherent sentence.

Phyllis had called Kevin to see if he would present the
award to me, and to her shock he had agreed immediately.
Then, just like that, there we all were.

Oh, yeah. I forgot something. Phyllis had invited my friend Rosie O'Donnell, too, who had also immediately agreed.

Now, this is when it gets fun.

Phyllis, being single at the time, seated Kevin, who was single at the time, at *her* table. She then went on to seat Rosie, who was also single at the time, at my table with Frank and the kids.

Now, I love Rosie and I'd enjoy having lunch with her any time, but NOT THIS TIME.

The menu was your standard chicken breast, rice, and spinach, but Cody and Cass were little so they had thoughtfully provided a kid's menu for them.

I kept looking over at Phyllis's table. Kevin's back was toward me, so I had no idea what was happening with him, but I could see Phyllis was in rare form, tossing her luxurious hair, laughing, stopping to ponder something profound Kevin had obviously just said, and smiling that magnificent Texas-size Miss America smile of hers.

Meanwhile Rosie kept eating the crust off my kids' grilled cheese sandwiches and giving them advice.

"Don't smoke crack," she said, stealing their french fries.

So far I don't think they have.

Anyway, the luncheon went on and on. Claudia and Phyllis gave great speeches. People ate. People clapped. People cried.

Then Kevin got up and gave the sweetest speech in the world, and I felt like Cinderella at the ball.

Finally I got up and thanked my hostesses, thanked Kevin for coming such a long way and saying such wonderful things, and then I finally remembered to thank my husband and children, whom I had temporarily forgotten existed.

Kevin Costner will do that to you.

The event ended successfully, and I went up to thank Claudia and Phyllis. Claudia beamed with pleasure. Phyllis was grinning like a woman in love. I mean, why not? She'd just spent three hours having lunch with Kevin Costner . . . *with a huge glob of spinach right between her two front teeth.*

Karma?

I'd like to think so.

P.S. Keep your girlfriends close and keep sexy movie stars where God intended them to be—at a theater near you.

If Frank had known what I was thinking about Kevin at that very moment, he wouldn't have been smiling.

FRANK AND I are shrinking. No doubt about it. I think it's unfair that you start to shrink exactly at the same time you can't lose weight anymore, can't get it up anymore, can't sleep anymore, can't see anymore, and can't hear a damn thing.

What?

Oh, sorry. I thought I heard you saying, "I know what you mean."

The Scope's Trial

I HAD MY FIRST COLONOSCOPY YEARS BEFORE I WAS TECHNICALLY supposed to have it.

I had been hearing a lot about colon cancer in the news, and it concerned me that even informed people such as Audrey Hepburn were not finding it in time to save their lives.

Now, Frank is the most proactive person I've ever known regarding his own health.

He goes to his gastroenterologist, Dr. Schmerin (that's right—his heinie doctor is named Dr. Schmerin), even before he needs to.

So years ago I agreed to have a colonoscopy because I wanted to prove to my father how easy it was. I wanted to prove it to Regis, too, who also refused to go for one.

Anyway, I soon discovered that the preparation for a colonoscopy is the tricky part, not the colonoscopy itself. In order to ensure a clean colon, you need to eliminate everything in it. Down to nada. Basically, you wind up with a very sore heinie.

Anyway, I held up Dr. Schmerin's scope the next morning on *Live* so I could explain to my daddy, watching at home on TV, how the procedure worked. Regis almost fainted, and my father absolutely refused right on the spot to even contemplate the notion.

But I later heard from hundreds of people that they decided to go and have a colonoscopy simply because I had lived to tell about it. Some of them found polyps and had them removed. Others found out the good news that they were A-OK for five more years until they should schedule it again.

Dr. Schmerin was very proud of me. I was clean as a whistle.

He's a doll, for a heinie guy.

P.S. It's important to have your scheduled colonoscopy exam, no matter who your heinie looks like.

P.P.S. I'm scheduled for my fourth colonoscopy next week. How the hell did twenty years go by so fast?

Who Nose Why God
Allows Such Suffering

OKAY, THIS IS THE BEGINNING OF THE END. TODAY, WITHOUT ANY warning, I discovered a gray hair . . . IN MY NOSE!

Nobody ever warned me about gray hairs in my frickin' NOSE! I'm growing gnarlier by the moment.

My descent into madness began the moment my friend Eva gifted me with one of those magnifying mirrors that blow up every pore to the size of the Grand Canyon. At first, you're so fascinated by the landscape of your own epidermis that you spend hours studying every nook and cranny you never knew you had. It's like a moonscape. You begin to pluck hairs as often and as efficiently as you can from places you never knew hair could grow. Then you realize that in your zeal to rid your visage of every offending follicle you have actually deforested your entire face. You no longer have anything that could credibly be called an eyebrow. It's like destroying the rain forest—

tree by tree. It's *gone,* and no amount of Sting and James Taylor concerts in Central Park will ever bring it back. You are
Jean Harlow. You now have McDonald's golden arches above
your eyes. The shame you feel upon realizing this is epic in
scope. Yet, still, the evil mirror beckons. Your tweezers tease
you. They know you want to. They know it's just a matter of
time and you'll be back.

"NO!" you scream. "I will not pluck! I *miss* my eyebrows."

And so for a while you're strong. You feel proud. You feel
smug.

"Yes! I am bigger than this!" you say to yourself.

But the truth is, you're not. Just a casual touch of your face
when you least expect it and there It is: where It did not exist
before. And It's thick and It's ugly and as unwelcome as a hemorrhoid.

And so, weak of will, you run for your trusty tweezers and
your beloved illuminator to dispense of your tormentor. Once
and for all.

And finally—savoring the moment—you pluck It. And
you flick It. You are triumphant.

Until in one last glance you realize—no! Could it be?
There, lurking in a sea of silent cilia—is the great-grandmother of all unwanted guests.

"Perhaps it's the angle of the sun that makes it shine like
that?" you try to convince yourself. Then you realize it is
DARK outside, and that's when the awful truth sets in: There,
right there, in your left nostril is a silver hair. You fall into despair because in your heart of hearts you know that even if you
pluck It, It will return. And It will bring friends. Many
friends. And they will have a Red Hat convention right there
in your nose. It's just a matter of what used to be my friend,
TIME.

Clowning Around

SOMETIMES I WONDER WHAT'S WRONG WITH ME. I HAVE NEVER liked parades, circuses, or roller coasters the way normal people do.

Maybe it's because I've been in show business all my life and show business is one nonstop roller coaster of a parade of circus acts. Maybe that also explains why I don't like monsters or clowns very much. They remind me of my agents. Just kidding.

But when I was about eleven years old and living in Maryland, I held a circus in my backyard to raise money for kids with muscular dystrophy.

The person who raised the most money got to go on television—WTTV channel 5 in Washington, D.C.—and give their check to a clown named Captain Tug. I was determined to raise the most money. So my brother, Dave, Michie, and I and the family dog, Zorro, put on a show.

We also had an auction, but the only thing of any value I had was my beloved Beatles album. The very first record they ever released. The one with their four faces. I was naturally reluctant to relinquish, it but I knew it would bring in the big bucks. So I went to my daddy and asked him if I should.

"You're trying to help kids by giving, right?" he asked.

"Right." I answered. "But how will I know when I've given enough?"

My daddy smiled his wise smile.

"When it hurts," he said simply.

Well, we raised $58.52 and won the right to present our money to Captain Tug.

A few weeks later we traveled to D.C. and I went on television for the very first time.

And guess who Captain Tug really was?

Willard Scott, that's who.

The fact that I'm still on television all these years later with a lovable clown named Willard Scott cracks me up.

But thank God for Willard. Otherwise I'd be the oldest person on the *Today* show.

Stay strong, Willard.

Stay very, very strong.

Laughter Is the Best Medicine

YEARS AGO WHEN I WAS DOING MY ANNUAL CBS CHRISTMAS SPEcials, I asked the network executives if I could have Carol Burnett on as a special guest. I was stunned when they told me no.

"Why?" I asked incredulously.

"She skews too old," they answered matter-of-factly.

"SHE MADE THIS NETWORK!" I countered. "She is the crown jewel of the Tiffany Network. CBS stands for *C*arol *B*urnett, *S*tupid!"

"That was years ago," they insisted. "We want you to have on some pop group that'll give us a younger demographic. You know, that skews younger."

I couldn't believe my ears, but they insisted. So we got *NSYNC.

The irony is that several years later Carol Burnett had a big reunion special on CBS and it got the highest rating of the season.

I was so happy for her and sent a note to congratulate her.

"Skew them!" I wrote. And she wrote back how funny she thought that was.

That is not the only time I made Carol laugh. Back in 2000 I took over for her on Tuesday night performances of the Stephen Sondheim Broadway musical *Putting It Together.*

Can you imagine the stress of trying to entertain people who are extremely disappointed that you are not Carol Burnett?

Well, one Saturday late in the run I got a call from Carol telling me she had pulled a muscle in her groin. I gave her the New York Giants' doctor's telephone number (it's good to have a former professional football player in the family) to get her some relief. He helped her out, but it became clear I was going to have to take over for her for several more performances. So I called her.

"Carol," I asked, "what do you want me to say on *Live* to the people who were hoping to see you? I mean, I can't very well tell them you got a groin injury, can I?"

"No," she said thoughtfully. "You probably can't say that, no."

I had an idea. "How about I tell them that you've pulled a muscle that leads to your vagina?"

I could hear Carol chuckling as she considered this.

"I know! I know!" I said. "I'll tell them you have a pussy pull!"

At that, I literally heard Carol fall off her bed, howling with laughter.

P.S. I'm aware it was a little risqué. But do you have any idea how good it feels to make the funniest woman on the planet laugh?

If not, I'm sorry, but skew you!

Dinner with Frank, Al, Oliver, and Two Very Nice "Friends"

You know those great *Where's Waldo?* children's books that are incredibly detailed, but hidden among the images you have to find Waldo? I can't tell you how many times I've thought to myself, "Uh-oh, I'm having a Waldo moment."

A couple of years ago Oliver Stone was planning on making a football movie with Al Pacino called *Any Given Sunday*. But they needed access to the real world of football to properly research the project, so they called Frank to help them navigate that rarefied landscape.

Now, Frank's been famous for more than sixty years. Me? A relatively short thirty years. So I'm still amazed when I answer the phone and there's a famous person on the other end. I mean, what do you say when the phone rings and a voice says, "Hi, it's Al Pacino. Is Frank there?"

Well, I'll tell you what you say. You say, "Sure, Al, let me get him for you." Then you hit the hold button and you scream, "FRAAAANK! It's AL friggin' PACINO."

Here's where Frank and I are fundamentally different: I'm *impressed* that Al Pacino is calling, and Frank is, well, NOT. It could be Elmer Fudd for all he cares.

So anyway, when he hangs up, I of course grill him about what could Al Pacino possibly want with Frank. Frank shrugs the Frank shrug and, being the long-suffering husband that he is, he calmly answers.

"He wants to have dinner. With Oliver Stone."

"OLIVER STONE!" I scream. Now I'm starting to think I was actually smart to marry Frank.

Dinner with Al Pacino and Oliver Stone! It beats a meat loaf with Ozzie and Harriet.

"Why?" I scream. "When are we going?"

The questions are coming at him like from a tennis ball machine. Once again Frank shrugs and says, "*We?* They want to talk football."

"I'll tell them everything I know!" I fairly shriek.

This at least makes Frank chuckle. That's always when I know I'm gonna get what I want.

We met for dinner at a delicious five-star restaurant.

Actually, we all arrived separately.

I had to attend an award ceremony across town beforehand. Frank had driven in from Connecticut and checked into a room in the hotel where the restaurant was located. Al was coming in from New Jersey, and Oliver was staying at a hotel downtown. And Oliver's dinner companions, a tall beautiful Russian woman and an equally beautiful shorter Latina woman, arrived right on time. Frank walked up to the reception area right after the maître d' had seated the ladies at the bar.

"Yes, Mr. Gifford," the maître d' said very professionally. "Two of your guests have just arrived. Please, follow me."

Well, Frank thought he meant Oliver and Al, but with one look at the exquisitely turned-out "guests," another idea occurred to him, and it was not a happy one. All he needed was a front-cover tabloid story featuring him here, apparently alone at a bar with two unusually gorgeous younger women.

He said, "Nice to meet you" and promptly excused himself with, "Oh, darn, I forgot something up in the room."

Suddenly my cell phone rang across town.

"Get over here!" he begged. "There seem to be two hookers waiting at the bar for me."

"Roger, buddy. Copy that," I replied. (Not really. I just thought that sounded funny.)

What I think I really said was, "Okeydokey, spumokey. I'm on my way."

The night was getting really interesting.

By the time I arrived at the restaurant, Frank, Al, Oliver, and his two friends were all seated there together in THE MIDDLE OF THE ROOM. There was not one eye in the restaurant that did not follow my every step to that table. I tried to act like I had dinner with Al Pacino and Oliver Stone and hookers every night. We all exchanged pleasantries and ordered some food, and once I got over their occupation, I found the two women to be surprisingly, well, normal. We talked politics, we talked food, we talked about everything under the sun except sex. I guess somewhere along the line we also talked football, but who cares?

All I know is that at the end of the meal, Al got into his car and went home to New Jersey, Frank and I went upstairs to our room, and Oliver Stone got into a very long limousine with two gorgeous women and went . . . well, wherever it is that Oliver Stone and two gorgeous women might go.

P.S. It didn't even make it as a tabloid item on Page Six. What's a girl gotta do?

It's Almost As If . . .

My mom is not dyslexic, but she's a bit dysfunctional in an adorable kind of way.

I mean, she reads just fine, but she often gets certain words or phrases confused. Like the first time she attempted to speak before a woman's Bible study group.

She was supposed to discuss the Syro-Phoenician woman but somehow ended up extolling the virtues of the Neo-Synephrine woman.

Or the time she meant to describe the Heimlich lifesaving maneuver but inadvertently called it the Heineken maneuver.

Don't even ask about the colonoscopy.

Anyway, you get my drift.

A few years ago my daddy, who was quite ill at the time, had to be manually lifted onto a private plane for his last trip home from Florida to Maryland. It was a terrible, sorrowful time for all of us, and tensions were running high. My mother and I had had an awful argument—the kind you can't remember the reason for years later. Nonetheless it was a doozy, and I'd resolved not to speak to her the whole way home. She'd done the same. We all boarded the plane. My daddy sat in the first seat looking forward. My mother took the seat opposite him, facing the rear of the plane.

Frank sat next to my daddy and I sat opposite Frank. The kids and whoever else was with us sat in the remaining seats toward the back of the plane.

I'm ashamed to admit this now, but Mom looked out her window and I looked out mine, both determined to remain silent in our own self-righteousness and resolve. Finally, about an hour later, my mother suddenly made a "Hmmph" sound.

I ignored it.

A few moments later she repeated it, louder and with a bit more emphasis.

"Hmmph," she said. "Look at *that.*"

I looked out her window.

"What?" I asked.

"Just look at *that,*" she replied.

"I did just look at *that,* and I didn't see anything."

"Hmmph," she insisted. "Look out *your* window."

I looked out my window. I saw clouds. The same clouds I'd been seeing for an hour and a half now. I wasn't amused.

"What are you talking about, Mom?" I demanded. "I don't see anything but *clouds.*"

"But *look* at the clouds," she insisted. "Look at the way they're *moving.* I mean, they're moving as fast as the plane."

I looked. "Mom, I'm sorry, but they look the way they've always looked."

My mother had had it with my attitude. "LOOK!" she screamed. "Why, it's as if we're flying *backward*."

"Mom," I answered, as nicely as I could, "YOU *ARE* FLYING BACKWARD!"

Suddenly—and thank you, God—*finally* she understood. She was indeed flying backward.

My daddy laughed so hard that he almost choked. And then we all did.

Laughed, I mean.

P.S. My mom is still flying backward. If you happen to run into her, please act like it's normal, and you fly backward, too. Thank you.

I'M A BIG BELIEVER in the power of prayer. Dementia runs in my family, so I keep praying that I won't forget how to pray that I won't get dementia.

You've Got Nail

I DON'T KNOW WHEN I BECAME OBSESSED WITH FINGERNAILS, BUT it must have been very early on because I can't remember a time when I was not obsessed with fingernails. I know it's shallow, but it's the first thing I notice.

Yes, I am deeply biased, highly prejudiced, and relentlessly judgmental when it comes to fingernails. So much so that if that were against the law, I'd be imprisoned for life. Maybe even given the death penalty. But this "Dead Woman Walking" would have a perfect manicure, I guarantee you. In fact, if it were a choice between a last meal and a last manicure—no contest. I'm going through those pearly gates *groomed*.

I'm a little more forgiving about toenails, but not much.

I watched the *Sex and the City* movie again recently, and all I could think was, "They're wearing dresses worth ten thousand dollars and they can't get a frickin' ten-dollar manicure?"

Then in the next scene you'd see somebody's foot in an eight-hundred-dollar Manolo Blahnik shoe with their ratty toes hanging out!

The irony is that ONLY THE SLUT, Samantha Jones, was freshly mani-pedied.

What? Oh, so that makes *me* . . .

Never mind.

Cougarrrr

DETAILS MAGAZINE HAS JUST COME OUT WITH AN ARTICLE CALLING me the craziest and sexiest woman on TV. I mean, I agree I am probably the craziest since Roseanne Barr left TV. But sexiest? To say I'm flabbergasted is an understatement. I think the young journalist who wrote the article is in serious need of some time on the couch. This guy's got real problems of an oedipal nature.

But it is strange for me to go from reading ten years ago that I was "the most dangerous woman in America" to reading that I'm suddenly "Daytime television's leading comedic cougar." It's surreal.

But it's all about perception. Do people really change? Or does change result from the environment that one finds oneself in? Have I remained the same and it's the world that's changed?

All I know is that with enough time on this planet, you do finally learn to differentiate between what's real and what's bull, and you finally feel free enough to express it.

The cougar part? That's interesting, too.

People sometimes ask me if I've ever been tempted to stray from the proverbial marital bed. That's easy. Of course I have. I'm old, but I'm human, baby. And I've still got one eye that sees pretty damn well. And sometimes it likes what it sees. But there are three reasons I don't go down that road:

1. My vows do mean a great deal to me.
2. I'm too tired.
3. What an idiot I'd feel like afterward. Because I've been an idiot many times in my life, and I don't like it.

Better to take a good look at what I've got and say a big prayer of thanks for it. And keep those fantasies under my pillow, where they're safe and sound and they never end up in the *National Enquirer.*

The Learning Curve

I NEVER GRADUATED FROM COLLEGE. I WENT TO COLLEGE. I STUDIED in college. I just left a little early, okay?

Now, Frank and I have always disagreed on the subject of education. But it's understandable why.

Frank lived in thirty-seven different places growing up before he finally got to Bakersfield High School when he was fifteen. I, on the other hand, sat in the same chair at the same desk with the same teachers for what felt like a lifetime.

He couldn't wait to stay put, and I couldn't wait to leave.

I remember my parents telling me about the European educational system, which is so different from our American one.

In the United States we give all high school students the SAT—Scholastic Aptitude Test—to determine a student's intelligence to qualify him for college. We just assume all children should go on to college. We expect it. In Europe, at the age of fourteen all students take a test to evaluate their knowledge and their *skills,* and then based on the outcome of the tests they are either sent off to university or they're sent off to a trade school to actually learn how to make a living.

I think the Europeans are on to something. There is a severe shortage of trained professional tradespeople and craftsmen in our culture, and way, way too many lawyers.

When one of my toilets is clogged up, I don't want some Summa Cum Laude showing up at my door. I want a Bubba Come Now-y with a big plunger! And when my power goes out, I don't want some Rhodes scholar explaining to me why $e=mc^2$.

I want some guy with a tool kit telling me, "Don't worry, Mrs. Gifford. I'm on it."

These people are heroes to me. They keep the sewers and the power lines safe for all of us. Even for college graduates who can tell you everything you ever wanted to know.

Except, of course, what you want to *hear:* "All fixed."

P.S. I propose a new test for all fourteen-year-olds. It's the EAT—*Employment* Aptitude Test.

P.P.S. Just a thought, and a darn good one at that. I mean, for a college dropout.

Ya Gotta Have Friends

IT IS SO GREAT TO HAVE FRIENDS THAT HAVE KNOWN YOU AND LOVED you since long before you became famous. But it's also great to make wonderful new friends because you already *are* famous, or infamous, as the case may be.

Such are our friends Mike and Lisa Kittredge.

Right after I left *Live with Regis and Kathie Lee,* Frank and I decided to put a home theater into our house in Nantucket. Our contractor told us that he had just built one for the Kittredges and that he'd be glad to call them in Europe and ask them if it would be okay to show us the results. They very graciously gave their permission. But they did have one request.

Apparently Lisa was a huge fan of *Live* and had loved my book, *I Can't Believe I Said That!*

By chance she had left it on the cocktail table in the living room and asked if I would sign it to her while I was there in their home.

So I signed her book and left a little note thanking them and leaving our Nantucket phone number in case they wanted to get together when they returned home.

That one "chance" encounter turned into one of the all-time greatest friendships we have ever had.

Mike is the founder of Yankee Candle and had just sold the company after battling cancer when we came into his life.

Mike and his wife, Lisa, are the kind of people who, though extraordinarily blessed materially, share absolutely every one of their blessings with others. Lots and lots of others. In the nine years that we have known them, they have built the world's most beautiful private yacht, *Paraffin,* and have had two gorgeous baby girls, Kylie and Kacey, and Mike has also successfully battled colon cancer two more times. In essence, he is a completely self-made extraordinary success story from very humble beginnings who has spent his whole life building dreams and taking others along for the ride. Literally.

The Gifford family has spent weeks and weeks on the high seas all over the world with this amazing family.

We have been to places we would never have gone to on our own—places such as Croatia and Iceland and Saint Petersburg, and others too numerous to mention.

And let me tell you, you really get to know people when you're confined on a boat—even a two-hundred-foot one like theirs.

Frank and I know lots of very successful people. You probably do, too. But the reason we love the Kittredges is because they still wake up every morning hoping to learn something new.

That's what keeps a person young at heart, I think—the desire to learn, explore new places, meet new people, and experience new worlds.

Now, granted, not everyone can do that in the lap of luxury. But Mike was a seeker and a dreamer long before he was a chemist who happened to have the brilliant idea of adding different scents to candles. The luxury came long after the heart was formed. My success came after my heart was formed, too. I still pray that on the day I die I will have just learned something I didn't know before. I want to die a student of life. See, I *do* believe in education. Especially the kind you get when you leave the classroom far, far behind.

Someday You're Gonna Be Dead

WE ALL HAVE FEARS. IN SOME WAYS GETTING OLDER IS AN ODD blessing because we've already faced some of our biggest fears and discovered that we're actually bigger than they are. We can look back over the shoulder of Father Time and see them knocked over and silent on the battlefield of life. It feels good.

But also with age comes wisdom. And even as gravity takes its toll on our thighs and buttocks, experience takes its toll on our hearts. There are still fears. Deep, aching fears.

How can I keep my children safe from harm? Especially now that they're leaving the nest to soar on their own? How can I stay healthy when so many of my friends and loved ones have fallen ill and died as a result of their illnesses? How can I safeguard my financial future in such a climate of economic disaster?

And, for me, how can I take care of my family if my husband passes away and leaves all the responsibility to me?

Even writing these questions sends a shiver of anxiety down my spine.

Frank and I are not rocket scientists. But we can do the math. When we fell in love, I was thirty-two and he was fifty-five. He was already a grandfather when we married five months later. He embraced my family and my emotional baggage, and I embraced his.

It wasn't easy but it was worth it. I look back on our nearly twenty-three years as a couple and breathe a huge sigh of gratitude that we're still together, our children are thriving, and we're all still healthy.

But I know that eventually our lives will change. "Lovers and lives always do" is a line I wrote a few years ago in a song called "An Old Friend."

So, you know what I do? I pray. All the time.

And then I laugh. I laugh a lot. About my wrinkles, my flop bags, and even death. Not because death is funny but because *life* is. And since we know we're all going to die eventually, why not spend each day laughing as much as humanly possible?

Laughter fills my life with joy, and joy equals strength—strength enough to face that biggest fear in the face and say: "Okay, I know you're going to win the battle someday, but today's not your day, and tomorrow doesn't look too good either."

Recently my longtime friend Alan Alda was a guest on *Today,* where he was promoting a new movie and the paperback publication of his most recent bestselling book. Alan and his amazing wife, Arlene, were guests at our wedding, and Frank and Alan had even appeared in a movie together many years before called *Paper Lion.*

We hadn't seen much of them lately, and so as Alan was leaving, I asked him, "Can we please at least have dinner together before Frank dies?"

Alan didn't miss a beat. In true Hawkeye Pierce tradition, he deadpanned, "Nah, let's do lunch after the funeral."

I screamed. He screamed. Even Frank screamed when I told him about it later.

We all "died laughing," you might say.

Yep. That's the way I wanna go.

Christine Maria Gardner Gifford Epstein

SOMETIMES THE BEST NEWS YOU'LL EVER GET COMES THROUGH THE mail.

It all started with a little note left in our mailbox back in 1988 when we lived in a 1760s farmhouse in the backcountry of Greenwich, Connecticut. Before Cody was born—or B.C., as we call it. I had been talking to Regis on *Live* about our adorable puppy, Chardonnay, that I was hopelessly in love with and worried about leaving when we went on location to tape our show.

When I got home later that afternoon, I discovered a small envelope in my mailbox addressed to me in the most beautiful handwriting.

The note inside was short, but I could tell that whoever had written it had a huge heart and a beautiful spirit.

Dear Mrs. Gifford,

Please forgive me for leaving this note in your mail-box but I heard that you were worried about your new puppy. My name is Christine Gardner and I just recently graduated from Fairfield University. I've lived in this neighborhood all my life and I would be happy to help you take care of Chardonnay while you're away.

Something about the sheer simplicity and sincerity of this girl touched my heart. I read it to Frank, and he felt the same way. Later I tucked the note away and said to myself, "I don't know why, but someday I'm gonna call her."

And eventually I did.

Christine was working at *Rolling Stone* magazine in New York City at the time.

She came to the house to meet with us, and we immediately loved her. It was impossible not to. She was always laughing, always smiling, and always completely responsible and dependable.

So for two years Christine house-sat and dog-sat for us whenever we went away.

You don't usually get to know a person when you're not together, but in this case, we actually did. Whenever we left, Christine was smiling, and when we returned, she was still smiling and so was Chardonnay. Hell, even the plants were smiling.

This could have gone on for years, except the unexpected happened: I got pregnant.

Nobody was more surprised than Frank and I. We'd simply gone on a Carnival Fun Ship vacation, and apparently we had indeed had a really fun time. All along the Amalfi Coast of Italy fun.

So now we needed to find a nanny because I intended to continue working before the baby arrived, and long after.

We considered an English nanny. We considered an Irish nanny. But we never really pursued either one.

Suddenly one day I had an epiphany.

"Frank!" I said excitedly. "Our nanny is right under our nose."

"What do you mean?" he asked, truly not understanding what I meant at all, which is not unusual.

"CHRISTINE!" I practically screamed. "She's *perfect*."

Frank had his doubts.

"Kathie," he argued, "Christine is a hip young girl who works at *Rolling Stone* magazine. Being a nanny is the last thing she'd want to do."

I wasn't anywhere near convinced.

"But, Frank," I countered, "being *our* nanny is a completely different thing from being some nanny stuck in the suburbs somewhere. This nanny is gonna see the world!"

Frank "Dubious" Gifford contemplated this.

"All right. Let's ask her. Invite her over."

So one fateful night Christine came over and we laid out the offer. Sort of like the army: JOIN THE GIFFORDS AND SEE THE WORLD.

Christine asked to think it over and let us know the next day. Reluctantly we agreed and went to bed hoping against hope.

Looking back now, the greatest day of our lives was the next day, when Christine uttered two letters: O.K.

She was there when Cody was born. She was there when Cassidy was born.

She has been there through every decision big or small, every breast-feeding, every school play, every public speaking event, every soccer, basketball, football, field hockey, and volleyball game.

She has been there for every report card, every doctor's appointment, every shot, every lost tooth, and every last chance to get that project done by tomorrow.

She has been the greatest blessing any family could possibly have. She made Mary Poppins look like an amateur. But then when the children got older, of course, everything changed.

When I left *Live,* we closed our New York offices and moved into a more convenient office near our home in Connecticut.

It was hard to say goodbye to Mickey, Gail, and Taryn, three incredible women in our office who had been with us through what I call "The Wars." But everyone set out on different paths, and we remain great friends to this day.

Eventually Christine morphed from being my children's nanny into being *my* nanny. She helped oversee my record company, my production company, my retail company, and all the in and out, day-to-day insanity of the Giffords' personal lives.

Recently I said to Frank, "I love you very much, honey, and I would miss you terribly if you ever left me. But if Christine ever leaves me, I WILL KILL MYSELF."

Frank just looked at me and smiled and said, "Me, too."

P.S. Thank you, Christine Maria Gardner Gifford Epstein from the bottom of my plaque-infested heart.

Head Case

I'M SURE IT SOUNDS UNUSUAL, EVEN SPOILED, TO MOST OF YOU reading this, but I was never completely alone with Cody until he was five months old.

We just have a very active household with tons of people coming and going and I've always been blessed to have an incredibly engaged co-parent in Frank and the unbelievably able nanny I just mentioned, Christine. Then when you factor in friends and a family that was always visiting, you begin to get the picture.

So, I was really looking forward to a particular Sunday in August when Frank was starting the football season, Christine was off, and no one was going to be home but Cody and me and our two dogs, Chardonnay and Chablis. Frank was doing some last-minute packing in our bedroom when I placed Cody in his little cloth chair on the kitchen counter and I began to prepare the puppies' breakfast.

"Mommy is so excited, Codes," I said, turning to put the dogs' dishes on the floor. "You and I are gonna have the best time together *ever*!"

That's when I heard the most terrifying thud I have ever heard.

Instantly I turned, and there was Cody. Facedown on the kitchen floor and screaming his brains out.

"Oh my God!" I screamed. "FRAAANK!"

Frank raced downstairs and found me cradling a very traumatized infant, bleeding from the mouth and dazed beyond belief.

Needless to say, everybody's plans changed. Frank and I rushed Cody to Greenwich Hospital, where Christine met us.

The guilt I felt was unspeakable, but I was so grateful that nobody made me feel even worse. Actually, I don't think I could have felt worse.

We spent hours in the emergency room while the doctors checked Cody out and finally sent us home. Cody was going to be okay, but he was going to have quite a scar on his chin.

Christine was as upset as we were so she came home with us, and Frank finally left to catch a much later flight.

I will never forget sitting there for hours with Cody lying in his bassinet on the floor between Christine and me. That's where I should have put him in the first place.

We just looked at him, and then looked at each other and cried and prayed all night.

The next day I went on *Live* and shared the whole incident with our audience, trying to warn everyone watching how dangerous those cloth chairs can be.

On my way home I stopped at the fish market on Green-wich Avenue to pick up something for dinner.

I was standing at the counter when a woman walked up to me, patted me on the back, and said "Don't worry, honey. I dropped mine on his head the day I brought him home," and promptly walked out the door.

P.S. I still love that woman.

It's hard to believe Cody was ever this little. Now his feet have their own zip code.

Eat Your Words

CASSIDY HAS MANY LOVELY QUALITIES, BUT NEATNESS HAS NEVER been one of them. Not that Cody is Mr. Clean. But I could put Cassidy in her crib at night freshly scrubbed from her bath, and somehow she would wake up with dirt under her fingernails.

How did she do it? She was *imprisoned* all night with no means of escape. But nevertheless, she always did. So it became accepted fact that Cass was our "Messy M'Cheany." One day Cassidy was especially enthusiastic chowing down her dinner. Cody was disgusted.

"Look at her, Mom! Look at Cassidy," he insisted.

I looked at Cassidy, who was, indeed, covered in spaghetti sauce.

"She's such a pig," Cody said.

"She is *not* a pig, Cody," I scolded him. "She's *precious*."

Cassidy the Great Philosopher ended the debate. Looking up from her meatballs, she announced "I'm a precious pig" and kept eating.

P.S. Years ago while in Colorado, Frank and I spotted a huge sculpture of a pig in an art gallery.

"Eat More Beef" was the title the artist had given it.

It now sits in our perennial garden patio in the backyard, keeping watch over every bite we take.

We just call her Precious.

An old-fashioned summer in Nantucket. Cass is six.

America the Bootiful

I'VE HAD SOME PRETTY GOOD GIGS IN MY LIFE, BUT SINGING THE national anthem at the Super Bowl pretty much takes the cake. In the fall of 1994, I got a letter from the NFL commissioner at the time, Paul Tagliabue, inviting me to sing in Miami a few months later.

This is the kind of thing you say yes to immediately before you have a chance to actually contemplate what the ramifications could be.

It's just such a huge honor that it would be downright un-American to say no.

Even so, I knew I'd get grief for it. I got grief for everything I did back then.

I said yes and decided I'd worry about catching grief when the time came.

See, I've learned that lesson the hard way. For too long I

used to fret and stew and toss and turn about something long before I had to, only to exhaust myself in the process. Then when the time would arrive to actually tackle the challenge, I would already be out of some of the steam I needed to rise to the occasion.

I prerecorded the anthem a month before in a studio in New York. Everybody prerecords it. The NFL insists on it because all the activities are timed down to a millisecond. Jet fighters are in the air scheduled to fly by the stadium at the precise time as part of the unbelievably finely orchestrated logistical nightmare that's beamed by satellite all over the planet. *That,* you try not to think about.

Barry Manilow had sung the anthem before, and he sent me the sweetest note. Basically it said, "Don't worry about it. You'll be great. Just make sure you don't look at the scoreboard, which tells you how many billions of people are watching you."

Ouch, huh?

So I made a mental note to avoid looking at the scoreboard at all costs. This was obviously before my eyesight went.

It was ABC's turn to broadcast the Super Bowl. Frank and the other *Monday Night Football* guys, Al Michaels and Dan Dierdorf, were scheduled to cover the game. There was some speculation in the press that Frank had lobbied his friends at the NFL for me to get the gig, but Frank would never have done that and Paul Tagliabue wouldn't have allowed him to, anyway.

Paul had heard me sing at the funeral of the former NFL commissioner, Pete Rozelle, several years before and thought of me for the gig.

Anyway, all of this seems very petty now and a million years ago.

I didn't buy a new outfit to wear. Even that morning I had no idea what I was going to wear. Eventually I picked out an old Escada navy-blue jumpsuit because it made me look patriotic without looking like Betsy Ross.

I really was amazingly calm. I mean, for a woman about to step into the biggest spotlight in the world before an audience that was still in awe of Whitney Houston's anthem just a couple of years before . . .

But you can't think like that, because it's a recipe for disaster. You should never try to be better than somebody else. You should always try, no matter what you do, to be the very best YOU you can possibly be. You'll never regret that. I had known years before that I would never be a world-class singer. So I tried to be a world-class performer who sang pretty well. That was more than sixteen CDs ago. Sixteen more than I ever thought I'd have made.

I did a sound check early in the day, and then they herded me off to some room inside the stadium for hair and makeup.

The next few hours were a blur, but then some production person showed up and said "final looks," which means whatever problem you've got, you're pretty much out of time to fix it. I didn't have any problem I could think of.

Until my makeup artist accidentally stuck me in my right eye with her mascara wand and my hairdresser accidentally sprayed hairspray in my left one.

They had to lead me onto the field like a blind sheep to the slaughter.

What can you do but pray at a time like that, which of course is exactly what I was still doing when I arrived at the microphone. Michie and Denise, my longtime friend and backup singer, smiled and gave me a big thumbs-up of encouragement. I was so glad they were performing with me.

I tried not to look at the crowd. But I could feel them. All seventy-five thousand of them.

And then it was time. No backing out. I heard Frank's voice on the PA system announcing, "To honor America with our national anthem, please welcome television star and Warner Brothers recording artist—and my wife—Kathie Lee Gifford."

I was a little annoyed about the "wife" part, but I knew he was just trying to be sweet.

Then, from somewhere far away, deep in the crowd, I heard something I had never heard before.

I heard boos. Not a lot of them but enough to wonder, "Why are people booing?"

But there was no time for an answer to that one. The orchestra was near the end of the intro and it was time for Mama to open her big mouth and lip-synch her brains out. So that's what I did.

And then jets were flying by and people were screaming and cheering, and suddenly big burly guys were rushing me off the field.

I later learned that a radio shock jock had suggested on his program that people should boo when they announced my name. I have no idea why. I've never met the man or listened to his radio show, but apparently he hated my guts.

I've always thought that the person doing the hating is the person with the problem, but that's just me. I've never made an enemy in my life, but if someone chooses to make you *their* enemy, what can you do?

Nothing, which is exactly what I did.

I flew home at halftime 'cause I had to be back on *Live* the next morning. It would have been nice to stay and watch the end of the game, but such is the story of my life.

Wham! Bam! And on to the next thing.

I honestly can't tell you who won the Super Bowl that year, although I think it was the San Francisco 49ers. I felt like I had won it by just getting through it in one semi-blinded piece.

Later someone told me what Jon Stewart had said on Comedy Central: "Well, it's been four days since Kathie Lee sang the anthem at the Super Bowl, and I still can't get my cat to come out from under the sofa."

Now, *that* I thought was funny, in a bootiful kind of way.

Talk Is Cheap

Giving your kids "the talk" is always a bit clumsy. But most experts agree you should do it before your child reaches nine years old.

I tried numerous times with Cody after he turned eight, but he was never too keen on the idea.

"Not now, Mom," he'd say. "I'm playing with my guys."

So I'd wait until Batman and G.I. Joe or the Power Rangers were finally done fighting, but by that time Cody was done, too.

Too tired for the birds and the bees. Pooped. So I'd wait for the next opportunity.

Then one day, just a couple of weeks shy of his ninth birthday, I closed the lid on the toilet, sat down, and said to him, midbath: "Okay, Codes. You're out of time. I want to be a good mother, and every book tells me we need to have 'the talk' while you're still eight. So we are going to have 'the talk' whether you like it or not."

Cody eyed me suspiciously, whacked two guys together very macho-like, and finally said, "All right."

And so I began.

As *spiritually* as I could, about how our bodies are gifts from God—temples of the Holy Spirit—how love between two people is a rare gift, how we're meant to compliment each other sort of like LEGOs, etc. He listened pretty well till I got to the technical part. It was too late to turn around, and I was determined to do my maternal duty. Plus, I didn't want Frank to do it and completely screw Cody up for the rest of his life.

I watched Cody's face go from the mildly interested to the somewhat surprised to the truly and totally repulsed. And then it was over.

I waited.

He said nothing.

I waited some more. He said nothing.

Finally, after what seemed an eternity, he pulled the plug and said, "Mom, can I watch *Rugrats* now?"

P.S. About six months later we were watching some movie where two people were kissing, and suddenly the music swelled romantically and the passionate image dissolved.

Cody looked at me and said, "That's not the end of the story, right, Mom?"

And then he winked at me.

Mission accomplished.

P.P.S. Ten years later I'm terrified I screwed Cody up for the rest of his adult life. Frank says I should've let him do it.

Only time will tell.

Keep This Up, Girlfriend

I AM THE PROUD GODMOTHER OF TWO BEAUTIFUL GIRLS. UNFOR-
tunately, they're on a reality series called *Keeping Up with the
Kardashians*.

Yep. Kylie and Kendall Jenner are Frank's and my goddaughters, and we love them very much.

I always told Kris, their mom, that their family would be
the perfect family to watch in a reality show. I mean, if life is a
three-ring circus, they certainly live under the big top, big-
time, all the time. Never a dull moment.

I actually encouraged my agent at William Morris to get
them a deal.

But eventually it happened without my help at all. It had
to. It's too unbelievable to be true.

You've got:

1. A beautiful mother with four kids, who marries
2. An Olympic hero father with four kids, whose best friend was
3. O. J. Simpson (accused murderer)
4. A sex tape (hey, who doesn't?)
5. Two more beautiful kids (my godchildren), and, finally,
6. Hollywood

I was happy for Kris when she first told me they had made a deal with Ryan Seacrest for him to executive produce their show on the E! channel. I love this family and I thought it would be great for them.

However, I felt the need to warn my friend about the perils she might face. "Be careful, Kris," I warned her. "You know TV these days. They aren't looking for *Leave It to Beaver*."

Okay, so that wasn't the best example. They *are* looking for that in a way—but you know what I mean.

Anyway, they shot the first season's shows, and we all waited for the premiere.

Cassidy, Christine, and I watched the first episode and sat there dumbstruck.

"What do you think, Cass?" I asked, hoping she had fallen asleep before it was over.

Cassidy didn't answer at first. Then she quietly and very honestly answered, "But they're not like that." She was absolutely right.

It was so uncomfortable. I wanted to share in my friend's good fortune, but I was so upset by the nature of the show.

A few days passed and Kris called to see what I thought. I couldn't lie to her. I told her Cass's reaction, and Kris got kind of quiet.

"Well, what do *you* think?" she asked me.

I took a deep breath, said a quick prayer that I wouldn't hurt this dear friend of thirty years, and said, "I think all the girls come off like sluts. I think Bruce comes off like an idiot. I think you come off like the worst mother in the world, and I think it doesn't honor the Lord in any way. Other than that, I liked it a lot."

Then we laughed, and she understood that even though I disagree with some of the decisions she'd made, I will never stop loving her. She is a great friend and a great girl and we've been through hell and back together.

Finally, as we were hanging up, she asked, "Any advice?"

"Yeah," I said, "please keep my goddaughters off that damn stripper pole."

P.S. *Keeping Up with the Kardashians* was the number-one-rated show that season on the E! channel.

IF I PRAYED as much as I pluck, I'd be the Dalai Lama.

If I were running for public office, I would run on an anti-flatulence platform.

If I had a nickel for every cork I've popped, I'd own the Betty Ford Center.

So, I guess when you put it all together:

I'd be the hairless and holy wine-soaked owner of the fart-free Betty Ford Center.

But. I wonder. Would I be happy?

OOOOH, YEAH.

P.S. It occurs to me upon rereading this page: What kind of a sick mind makes up this stuff?

Daddy's Girls

Awhile back I had an idea for a sitcom I thought was a scream.

Remember John Derek? He was married to Ursula Andress, dumped her for Linda Evans, and then dumped *her* for Bo Derek.

Well, I thought a takeoff on that premise would be hysterical. I called it *Daddy's Girls.*

Basically, a talent manager, "Daddy," falls in love with a voluptuous country singer (Dolly Parton) at the Grand Ole Opry, then dumps her five years later for a Broadway singer (me), and dumps *her* five years later for a Vegas showgirl (Marilu Henner), whom he dumps—you got it, five years later.

Finally he marries a hot Latina singer (think Shakira) and dies of a heart attack on his wedding night because he overdosed on Viagra.

Okay, hysterical so far, right?

Only Daddy had drunkenly made a will the night before the wedding with his best man, his attorney, saying that in the untimely event of his passing, ALL FOUR of his wives would inherit his Beverly Hills estate and live happily ever after. So it was sort of a multi-musical genre *Golden Girls*.

None of that is really important except that it brought Marilu and Dolly, our agent, Sam Haskell, and me together several times for creative meetings. I'm crazy about both of these ladies. They are completely different, but real survivors in this industry.

One day both of them showed up for lunch at my house in Connecticut to discuss the idea.

Dolly will eat anything, but Marilu is very particular. So I basically ended up serving pig's feet for Dolly and tofu and hummus for Marilu.

While we were eating, we couldn't help but reminisce about the past. Spirits were flying as we all shared stories.

I don't remember why, but for some reason I shared some gynecological experience.

"I just hate having my legs up in the stirrups," I told them. "I don't think there's a woman in the world who likes it."

"I do!" Dolly virtually screamed, and went on to regale us with anecdotes about her and her gynecologist, who she thought was a real dreamboat.

Later we went into my backyard to take a picture to capture the memorable moment.

Dolly took one look at Precious, the pig sculpture in our garden, and promptly mounted him, saying, "I've ridden a lot of pigs in my day, but nothin' this hard!"

She might be my favorite woman EVER.

Well, we just had the best afternoon, but I knew that any

moment the kids would be coming home from school, and I was nervous about it. Why? I'll tell you why. Because Cody, who was eight at the time, was absolutely in awe of Dolly's mammaries, that's why. I know, I know. Who isn't?

But I had spent days preparing Cody for Dolly's visit.

"Cody Gifford, you are not to look anywhere but into Dolly's *eyes*. You got it? 'Cause if you don't, I'm gonna bust your butt."

"Yes, Mommy," he'd answered sheepishly. But I had my doubts. Well, suddenly I could hear Cass arriving in the kitchen.

"Casserole!" I yelled to her. "Come on out and say hello to Marilu and Dolly."

She came right out and walked up to Marilu and shook her hand and said, "Nice to meet you." And then she turned and walked up to Dolly's boobs and said right into them, "Nice to meet you, too." It had never occurred to me to warn *her*.

We all screamed, and that's when I heard Cody's voice in the next room.

"Cody," I called out to him, "come on out, sweetheart."

"No, thank you, Mom" is all I heard.

Annoyed, I repeated my command a little more sternly.

"Do I have to?" he asked meekly.

"Yes, you do, and you better make it now."

Well, I must have scared the hell out of him in the days preceding, because he pretty much backed into the room to avoid coming face-to-face with the twin peaks. He finally got close, looking down at his feet, and said "Nice to meet you" to both of the women.

"Oh, Cody," Dolly cried immediately. "You are just *precious*!" And then she swooped him up into her arms and hugged him, pretty much smothering his face in the forbidden kingdom.

"Let's play the piano, honey," she said, and laughed, dragging him to the baby grand and patting the piano stool, encouraging him to sit next to her.

What could the poor kid do?

I will never forget the image of Dolly bouncing exuberantly next to him as her three-inch fingernails pounded those ivories and they played "Heart and Soul." I couldn't tell whether Cody wanted to die or live forever.

Dolly'll do that.

P.S. I still think it's a great idea for a sitcom. But what do I know? Probably "skews" too old.

One of my favorite days ever. Marilu and Dolly came to visit me and Precious the Pig.

Miss Manners

I THINK TEACHING YOUR CHILDREN TO SHARE WHAT THEY HAVE with others is one of the most important, most valuable lessons parents can impart. Human beings are born selfish and remain selfish for the rest of their lives unless someone teaches them otherwise. We come out of the womb wanting stuff and spend whatever time on this earth we have *getting* stuff, often by *taking* stuff away from other people who have stuff we *want*.

This is not nice. This is why we have wars.

And this is why I have been an absolute maniac about teaching my children manners since before they could say "Give it to me, Big Mama."

If they wanted something, they did not get it until they said "please." If they did not say "thank you" after they got it, I took it away and we'd start all over again.

It was a battlefield for a while but well worth every single battle. I remember when Frank would leave on Sundays to host *Monday Night Football*. He'd be gone until Tuesday, so Cody loved being the man of the house till Daddy got home.

He'd snuggle in bed with me most nights, and invariably he'd have to get up to go potty several times. Eventually even at his sleepiest, his absolute drowsiest, he'd say, "I need to go pee-pee, peese, Mommy."

"Okay, Codes," I'd respond, and gently lead him to the toilet, where he'd hit everything but the toilet. (Hey, it was dark.) Then I'd guide him back to my bed and he'd snuggle right back in and say "Tank oo, Mommy" and fall promptly asleep. Years later when President Bush got out of that jet fighter and announced "Mission accomplished," I knew exactly what he meant.

Well, after Cassidy was born, we started the whole process all over again. By now she had a big brother who was a pretty good role model for her, at least until he became a teenager.

Cassidy actually became very competitive in the manners department. If a waitress brought her anything, she'd say "thank you" before the plate hit the table.

If the waitress didn't say "you're welcome" immediately, she'd say "thank you" a little louder, thinking perhaps the waitress hadn't heard her the first time. This would sometimes go on four or five times until the flummoxed waitress would finally yell back, "All right already. Geez, kid, you're *welcome*."

To this day she's the Manners Monster in our family, and as recently as yesterday when I reached for something, asking "May I?" she scolded, "May I *please*? Geez, Mom."

I have created an extremely polite pain in the ass.

One day when Cass was about three years old, twelve of

us were having lunch at a restaurant called, appropriately enough, Cassidy's, in Avon, Colorado.

Everybody ordered, and eventually all the food arrived. There was a veritable plethora of thank-you's from everyone, let me tell you. After about five minutes Cass got up and started going around the table, giving her french fries away to everyone, one by one. By the time she was finished, she was out of french fries.

"Cassidy!" I exclaimed. "I am *so proud* of you! I can't believe how precious you are. You are so good at *sharing,* honey. You gave all your french fries away."

Cassidy looked at me like I was a moron and said, "I done want dem."

Oh.

Battle of the Sexes

One day I took Cody and Cass to lunch at Terra, one of our favorite restaurants in Greenwich.

They were probably about eight and four at the time.

Cody, naturally, took out all his Power Ranger guys to battle as we waited for our food.

Cassidy, naturally, took out her Barbie and Ken dolls to kiss and cuddle while she waited, too.

They both played quietly for a long time, lost in their respective worlds, maneuvering their different toys this way and that into whatever situation they imagined. Eventually all of Cassidy's dolls were coupled together and all of Cody's were facedown on the table.

Finally Cassidy said, "Look, Mama. They're all in love."

Cody, not to be outdone, said, "Look, Mom, they're all *dead.*"

I don't care what anyone says. Boys and girls are different, and I for one say, "*Vive la différence!* And pass the Parmesan cheese."

"Oh, sorry, Cass. *Please* pass the Parmesan cheese. Thank you. You're welcome." *Grazie.* Whatever.

Good grief. I'm exhausted.

What Is a Family?

IF YOU VISIT OUR HOME IN CONNECTICUT (AND SOMEDAY I HOPE you do, but not all at once), chances are you will be greeted by two of the most adorable little girls you have ever seen. No doubt you will wonder who they are and why they are there, because they do not look like Frank or me, and they definitely don't look like the mailman.

Let me explain.

When Frank and I first fell in love with our vacation home in Colorado in 1993, we met an extraordinarily polite, hard-working young Hispanic American named Andy Medina. He was born and raised in Colorado under very tough circumstances, but he was as likeable a young man as you would ever hope to meet.

At that time Andy was the reservations manager at the Cordillera resort, where Frank and I had recently bought a mountaintop home. Andy picked us up at the airport and, during the course of the long drive from Denver ended up showing us the engagement ring he had yet to offer to Elvia Romos, the beautiful young Mexican woman he had fallen in love with and hoped to marry.

It was so sweet and so life-affirming to be around everything that is right and good about the young. The two of them just exuded hope and promise.

Well, you can guess what happened next. Yep, just like Christine, Andy and Elvia became what we call "lifers"—people who have become so dear to us, so deeply embedded in our lives, that we don't remember where their family line ends and ours begins.

Andy and Elvia lived in our home in Colorado until we finally asked them to move to our main home in Connecticut and help us with the growing needs of our family and increasingly complicated lives.

They agreed, but their lives were complicated as well. For years Elvia had been working toward acquiring her American citizenship. Just marrying an American was no longer enough, because of so much corruption in the immigration process.

Well, finally, she did indeed receive her citizenship in 1995, just as I was scheduled to sing at the lighting of the Christmas tree in Washington, D.C.

I invited Elvia to come with us to the event, and she eagerly agreed. I mean, she is one of twelve children from a poor family in Aguascalientes, Mexico, who had barely seen the world, much less the view from inside the Oval Office.

I sang a couple of numbers at the ceremony, and then we all went to the holiday party at the White House, which was like walking into winter wonderland on Christmas Eve. Cody and Cass were hungry and ready to boogie.

But first we all stood in line to shake the president's and first lady's hands. Elvia was all "atingle." She just beamed as she stood next to Bill Clinton and the photographer snapped her picture with the president of the United States of America.

A week later Elvia sent out her Christmas card, with the picture of her standing next to Bill Clinton, to all her friends and family in Mexico.

Under the picture it said: "Hola, everybody. Made it to America. Have made many nice new friends."

Well, the party was a gas. Santa Claus was really a Secret Service agent who was doing double duty that night. Cassidy, age two, took a particular liking to him and insisted that he dance every last dance with her.

Finally, at the end of a very long evening, Santa came up to me, bedraggled with his beard askew and his suit asunder.

"Mrs. Gifford," he panted, "I have been trained for any emergency—any terrorist attack imaginable. But nothing in my life has trained me to deal with a two-year-old."

We all returned to Connecticut the next day, where Andy and Elvia eventually began to make babies of their own.

First came Julia Emma, now seven. And then came Isabella Sophia, now three.

These would be the two little faces that would greet you at our door if you visited us today.

Along with my other two children, whom I love just as much.

Most of the time.

It's a Dog's Life

I LOVE DOGS. SOME PEOPLE ARE CAT PEOPLE OR HORSE PEOPLE OR gerbil people or fish people, but I've never been anything but a good old-fashioned dog person.

Frank was in no hurry to have children when we first got married in 1986 because he already had three children by a first marriage. In fact, three of his grandchildren were at our wedding. So instead, to buy some time, he got me a puppy. A precious little bichon frise named Chardonnay.

Well, she was such a hit that we ended up getting a bichon for my niece, my brother, my backup singer, and Cassidy's godmother, Laurie, all from the same mother. But then Laurie thought her German shepherd would eat her bichon, Chablis, so we ended up keeping her, too.

Chardonnay was a terrific watchdog. "Chard on Guard" we called her.

Chablis was a terrific eater. "Chab the Flab" is what we called her.

Both dogs were waiting when we brought our children home from the hospital after they were born.

Now, Regis had publicly begged me to name our son after him, but I had absolutely refused.

"No!" I always told him. "I can't believe your parents named *you* that."

When we found out that our second child was going to be a girl, he begged me again.

"Please name her Regina!" he insisted.

"Absolutely not," I responded again, and I meant it.

He was devastated. At least that's what he said. So finally I said to him, "Look, if I rescue some puppy from the pound somewhere and name it Regis, will you finally get off my back?" I was half kidding.

"You would do that for *me*?" he asked, genuinely thrilled.

So a few weeks later we played the Doggy Dating Game on *Live,* and I had to ask three puppies questions and, depending on their responses, choose one of them to adopt.

It was no contest. This precious little mutt of questionable heritage looked into my eyes and it was all over. I was in love.

The other two dogs got adopted, too, but Regis Champagne Gifford came home with me.

He had the mange and a bad case of fungus, but about ten thousand dollars' worth of veterinarian bills later he was good as new.

He's fourteen years old now and has been the best dog you could ever hope to have.

But best of all, I just loved saying, "Regis, get off the couch." Or "No, Regis, don't you dare poop on the carpet."

The January after my daddy died was unusually frigid.

We live on a peninsula that juts into the Long Island Sound, and for the first time anyone could remember, the sound froze solid for about two weeks.

One afternoon I came home after picking Cassidy up from school and instantly sensed something was wrong.

Regis and Chablis were in their usual spots in the mudroom. Chardonnay was nowhere to be found, and my heart just froze. We searched everywhere.

Finally we found a spot on our property where an obvious struggle had taken place. Fresh blood was evident on the snow.

I ran to the west side of our property and looked out onto the frozen sound. And there she was, lying so still that my heart stopped. I didn't care if the ice cracked underneath me, I raced out onto the surface and gathered Chardie into my arms, sobbing into her lifeless body as I carried her home.

A coyote had killed her and then attempted to drag her back to its den across the cove. But Chardonnay had been wearing one of those "invisible fence" collars that had gone off when the coyote had crossed the property line, and I guess it had shocked him. He'd dropped her and run away, stunned and, thankfully, still hungry.

Chard on Guard had been doing what she did best: protecting her family from intruders.

I'm still not over it.

Later that year in June we left for a vacation in Europe. Frank received a phone call while we were on the Kittredges' beautiful boat on the Riviera, but he didn't tell me about it until we were almost home because he knew it would have ruined everyone's trip. It seems we had barely left our driveway when Frank's son, Kyle, who lives with us, had backed his car out of the garage and accidentally run over Chablis, killing her instantly.

So we lost my daddy and Chardonnay and Chablis all

within a year, and it was devastating for everybody. Regis just moped around missing his sisters so badly that he wouldn't eat. We all worried that he would die from a broken heart.

So when Cassidy asked for a new puppy a year later, we immediately agreed. Regis needed a buddy. And we all needed someone new to love, too. Cass had her heart set on a Malti-poo so we drove up to Milford, Connecticut, where we'd been told we could find one.

But instead we found another bichon that Cass named Louis.

Louis changed the whole dynamic in our home. Regis became a puppy again. We all did.

And I've never seen Frank adore a dog so much.

"He looks you right in the eye," Frank loves to say. "Most dogs won't do that."

I think Frank also respects that Louis is the finest canine athlete he has ever seen. Louis can jump higher than Kobe Bryant. He just stands there and leaps through the sky and lands wherever he wants. It's amazing. Louis and I bonded in a very special way, too. I think it's because I wrapped up all my accumulated grief and poured it all out by loving on him.

I could never put him down. I rubbed him and kissed him and rocked him like a newborn. And he loved back the same way. He just ate it up.

But he didn't handle my absences very well. He'd watch me leave with the biggest, saddest brown eyes you've ever seen.

One day I came home after a long day and our beloved housekeeper, Gloria, met me at the door.

"Mrs. Gifford," she said worriedly, "I have to show you something. It's very sad. But it's very funny."

I couldn't imagine what could be sad but funny at the same time, but I soon found out.

She led me into the dining room, where all the chairs were perfectly pushed in under the table.

"What, Gloria?" I asked, looking around.

"There," she said, pointing.

And there it was. A huge, perfectly formed Dairy Queen circular turd on top of the dining table, more than three and a half feet up from the floor.

You gotta admire a dog that can jump that high and leave such a strong declaration of his feelings.

Two years passed and we all got on with our lives. Regis and Louis became inseparable. All was well.

And then right after I joined the *Today* show in April 2008, Frank and I attended a fund-raiser for an organization called Life Athletes. It had been founded by Frank's dearest friend, Wellington Mara, who had signed Frank to the Giants back in 1952.

Well had recently died, and Frank and I tried to spend as much time with his beautiful wife, Ann, as we could.

I have to admit, I really didn't want to go that particular night. I had just started working full-time again and I wasn't into a routine yet.

"Just come to the cocktail reception and say hello to Ann," Frank suggested. "I'll stay for the program and you can excuse yourself and go home to bed."

That had been the plan until the very first moment we walked into the ballroom, and I saw a group of nuns and priests crowded around a young woman with an unbelievably gorgeous golden doodle in her arms.

That puppy looked at me, and I walked right up to it, cradled it to my flop bags, and said, "I don't know who you are, but you are coming home with me tonight."

It turns out that the puppy was to be auctioned off that evening to benefit the Life Athletes charity.

Frank looked at me like a deer in the headlights.

"Absolutely not, Golda," he said, shaking his head for emphasis.

Just calling me Golda was emphasis enough. That's what he always calls me when he is extremely perturbed.

"Yes, Frank!" I insisted. "Regis is failing and Louis is going to need a sister. We are supposed to adopt this puppy and bring her home."

"*Tonight?*" he exclaimed through clenched teeth. "Absolutely not. No way. Forget it."

Well, I held that puppy for hours until the auction began. By then I had every nun and priest praying that Frank would change his mind and that we would secure the winning bid.

Finally Frank caved in and joined the cause, just like I knew he would. Then, just as the auctioneer was about to yell "Sold!" I lifted up my hand and bid a thousand dollars more than Frank.

He looked at me in utter disbelief.

I laughed and hugged his neck. The puppy licked him.

"Sold!" The hammer came down, and with that she was ours.

The owner had already named her Lola, which by coincidence was also Frank's mother's name—Lola Mae Hawkins.

So we felt it was only right to keep calling her Lola. But what about her middle name?

I looked over at Ann Mara, who had prayed the hardest for me.

"Mara," I said to Frank. "Wellington would love that." Lola Mara Gifford.

So that night, many hours and one puppy later than I had planned, we headed home.

Regis was annoyed. Louis was suspicious, and the kids were surprised.

But thank goodness Louis didn't take his feelings and deposit them on the dining room table.

He's been watching Dr. Phil and knows better now.

P.S. Our beloved Regis passed away on October 2, 2008. He died peacefully in Frank's arms, and we will forever be grateful for such a loyal, loving friend.

Lola's (center) first morning at the Gifford home. Regis (left) wants nothing to do with her and Louis (right) is understandably depressed. But Frank, as usual, is going with the flow.

Time Out

My son, Cody, is off to college now, and not a moment too soon. For years I couldn't bear to let him out of my sight. Nursery school was agony, but now I'm counting the days.

What happened?

Everyone tells me it's natural, normal, and *necessary* for a male child to distance himself emotionally from his mother.

Distance himself *how far*? That's what I wanna know.

It all started around the age of fifteen, when I noticed I no longer got hugs and kisses in the morning. I got, "HHUUMU." That's it. "HHUUMU."

I'm sorry, but I truly do not know how to spell what I got from him, but suffice it to say it was a shock to my system.

Over time I noticed that NOTHING I said was remotely important. In fact, it became painfully clear that it was a miracle of God that someone as stupid as I had actually been able to make something of herself.

Once he reached six feet four inches, it was impossible for me to tell him anything at all.

One school night I was trying to get Cassidy to get to bed, when Cody came busting through her door, testosterone in tow. And volleyball in hand.

It was RUMBLE TIME!

"No, Cody," I said. "It's bedtime." I reached out to push him on his way. All he did was hold up his arms to deflect me, and he broke my ring finger. Just like that. Broken.

I am now wearing a hundred-dollar fake diamond ring where my quite costly ring once sat because my finger is swollen to twice its normal size. Why?

BECAUSE IT'S TIME.

That's why.

Crunch Time

THERE WAS A TIME IN OUR LIVES WHEN IT FELT LIKE WE COULDN'T go anywhere without being accosted by paparazzi and all the ensuing craziness. We learned how to adapt, but it wasn't easy.

"Cody," I used to tell him, "the whole world is watching us. If you're going to act up, you act up at *home,* where I can beat the crap out of you without anybody knowing." (Reader, if you don't realize that I'm kidding by now, we have a serious problem.)

It seemed like a good idea at the time. But, can I tell you the crazy truth?

That's exactly what he did. This now hulking six-foot-four-inch kid who had broken my finger was also a model student and a model athlete. He even starred with me in a Disney movie called, *Model Behavior.*

One night when we were filming in Toronto, we were waiting to shoot a scene. It was getting really late—like two A.M. late—and I was getting very concerned that Cody had been waiting for hours in full makeup and full wardrobe to finally film his scene.

I'm as patient as a saint when *I'm* waiting to work, but I'm a lioness in heat when it comes to my kids. I kept going to the back of the trailer to check on Cody to see if he was okay.

I'll never forget it. The very first Harry Potter book had just come out, and Cody was totally engrossed in it.

"Codes," I asked, "are you all right waiting, honey?"

Cody looked up at me and said, without a hint of hesitation, "Mom, this is a privilege for me" and promptly went back to his book.

He was nine years old. He hit his marks, he said his lines, he never caused an ounce of trouble. BECAUSE HE SAVED ALL HIS TROUBLE FOR HOME!

He even thanked the director and the crew when we wrapped.

Years later when he graduated with a 4.2 GPA in high school and grunted at me over his Banana Nut Crunch, I remembered what I had told him.

As Stephen Sondheim famously wrote, "Careful the things you say. Children will listen."

THE OTHER DAY I noticed a bruise on Frank's lower lip.

"What happened to your lip?" I asked.

"What about it?" he asked me back.

"It's bruised," I said.

"Oh, I had a piece of corn," he remembered.

"It looks like when you used to devour *me*," I observed.

Frank shrugged. "I prefer corn now."

P.S. Me, too.

Political Folly

I AM A TOTAL NEWS JUNKIE AND I AM ABSOLUTELY FASCINATED BY politics, but I really despise what politics do to otherwise intelligent, rational, and normally decent human beings. Like my husband, for instance.

Frank and I agree on many things, but we're miles apart on others. He's a die-hard compassionate conservative, and I'm a bipartisan independent who veers widely, depending on the issue. Truth is, I have a big problem with the crazy people on the radical extreme of both parties. I don't want to belong to either of those clubs because crazy people scare me. Frank and I are usually all right until we happen to have lunch or dinner with someone who refuses to even contemplate anything that questions or refutes the far left's stand on any issue.

Now, I know that John Wayne has been dead for years, but

don't tell Frank. Because John Wayne comes to life again in the form of Frank Gifford every time this happens.

I'm not kidding. Frank *morphs* into John Wayne and he loses all resemblance to the calm, measured Adonis I fell in love with twenty-three years ago.

I try to sense when it's coming, try to defuse the situation with humor, try to deflect attention—*anything*. But it's to no avail. John Wayne is on his horse, guns blazing, and he doesn't care if you are General Santa Anna and the Mexican Army at the Alamo. He is not going to go out without a fight.

A lot of it is because he's lived so long and seen so much. He was a marine during the Korean War. He just doesn't "suffer" what he calls fools too well.

Of course the poor schmuck on the receiving end of John Wayne's fury doesn't think much of the Duke during these episodes, either. All it adds up to is a very expensive meal that nobody enjoys. It makes me crazy. I mean, what happened to that friendship that mattered so much you both took time out of your incredibly busy schedules to make a date in the first place? It's often a very quiet trip home. Frank is completely sure he did nothing but stand up for his God-given, constitutionally guaranteed right to his opinion, and I'm wishing like Rodney King that we could all just "get along." Because, to me, our common ground is our *sacred* ground.

The crazy thing is, just when you are absolutely convinced that the friendship is over, one offended party or the other calls and makes another date for lunch or dinner.

And, of course, for old times' sake, we climb into the car to go meet them—hope springing eternal that this time it will all turn out hunky-dory.

But let me tell you something. As long as John Wayne is

alive and well and living out his days at our house, I wouldn't put money on it. Especially during an election year.

Giddyup, Duke!

P.S. Barack Obama is our new president, and I'm proud to say that Frank has calmed down a great deal. But he's still very suspicious about Charles Krauthammer. And he should be.

A Dinner Date with History

As much as I'm privately caught up in politics, I rarely get involved publicly, and I never campaign for any one candidate. It's just such a personal decision for people and so divisive in our culture.

But I have made the rare exception and lobbied for legislative change when I truly felt an injustice was so grievous that I had to try to change it.

Such was the case in 1995.

Frank and I were guests at Claudia Cohen's beautiful estate in East Hampton that summer. Claudia was dating Senator Alfonse D'Amato at the time, who also happened to be a close friend and adviser to then New York governor George Pataki.

Claudia had invited the governor and Mrs. Pataki to dinner one particular evening, and I was nervous and excited about having the governor all to myself for a couple of hours. Claudia was in on my plan and graciously seated the governor to my right and Frank to my left.

Why was I nervous? Because the Association to Benefit Children, a charitable foundation that we are heavily involved in, was in the middle of suing the state of New York over the blinding of HIV testing for pregnant women.

Why was I excited? Because I had news I truly believed could settle the case favorably, and Governor Pataki was the key.

Through our work at the Association to Benefit Children we had learned that if a pregnant woman who was HIV-positive received a cocktail of certain drugs during her pregnancy, the chance of her giving birth to an HIV infant went from 40 percent down to less than 8 percent.

Now, the government had been testing women in clinics for years and sending the results to the Centers for Disease Control in Atlanta simply to track the progress of the AIDS epidemic.

BUT THEY KEPT THE TEST RESULTS PRIVATE, never informing the woman or her physician of her status.

We felt that this was obscene. Like withholding the cure for cancer. So the Association to Benefit Children, through our great friend Gretchen Buchenholz, was suing the state of New York to unblind the tests.

Here was my chance to educate the governor, whom I truly believed had no idea of these startling statistics. Very few people did.

So in between courses I basically plowed into my pitch with very little champagne pleasantry.

To his credit, Governor Pataki listened to me quietly and politely. He ate while I talked and gave no indication of how this information was going down with his Chilean sea bass.

Finally I was finished.

And to my astonishment George Pataki said three things you rarely hear a politician say:

1. I had no idea.
2. We're on the wrong side of this issue.
3. I'm going to do something about this immediately.

Dinner ended and I thanked the governor (and Claudia) profusely, but I still had my doubts about his sincerity.

One month later Governor Pataki issued an executive order that the state of New York would unblind the HIV test results of pregnant women immediately and inform all patients and their doctors of the results. The lawsuit was dropped.

It was a stunning reversal of policy and one heck of a miracle, too. But it was also incredibly controversial.

I remember standing with the governor before the New York City press corps in the memorial garden of Cody House on Ninety-first Street as the governor read his proclamation. In the distance I could hear a crowd chanting.

"Governor Pataki, we have rights, too. Governor Pataki, we have rights, too!"

Personally, I could not imagine anyone who would oppose the alleviation of children's suffering, but there they were, trying to make the evening news.

Basically it was a privacy issue: Some gay lobbyists were against the unblinding of the test results because they felt it would lead to persecution of HIV-positive gay men in the workplace. Now, I'm all for gay rights. But I'm also all for *human* rights, and that includes children's rights, and until gay men can get pregnant, I thought they should step aside from the issue so that children might benefit.

Governor Pataki did a powerful, courageous thing in a politically charged city, and he is to be commended for his willingness to turn a deaf ear to those who opposed mercy.

One year after the unblinding of the CDC tests, the AIDS death rate went down for the very first time in New York. Because the AIDS *birth*rate went down.

Soon after, the policy was adopted all over the country, and it still stands today.

Governor Pataki will always be one of my heroes.

It's simple.

It was the right thing to do.

The Donald to the Rescue

Most people who would die to have fame and fortune have no idea how you can die *from* fame and fortune.

It looks too good to be true because it is.

I was scheduled to host the Miss America Pageant with Regis in September of 1993, just six weeks after Cassidy was born. So I breast-fed her for five weeks, pumped one week's worth of milk, and then wrapped those puppies in ice-cold cabbage leaves to shrink them back into a size-four dress.

It was tight, but we did it.

Cass was clean and weaned when we got on Donald Trump's helicopter to fly to Atlantic City for the pageant. Frank was on location somewhere for *Monday Night Football* so he had called Donald to see if his security guys would keep an extra eye out for us. Donald had graciously offered us his helicopter to take us on the forty-minute trip.

When we arrived, we were greeted by two burly body-guards, who remained by our sides throughout the week of rehearsals.

Suddenly I seemed to be surrounded by a sea of security, but I chalked it up to Donald's generosity.

Until the morning of the pageant, when I went downstairs in the hotel to buy a newspaper.

"KATHIE LEE DEATH THREAT" was the blaring headline of the *Daily News*.

I couldn't believe my eyes. Naturally, I had a vested interest in reading the accompanying story, so I quickly paid for the paper and rushed upstairs to read it.

It was almost surreal: A man in North Carolina was obsessed with me. He had kidnapped, raped, and tortured his aunt and then had stolen her car, intending to drive up to Connecticut and find me, and God knows what he was going to do next. But he left the car in a Virginia airport parking lot, where it was discovered. The FBI contacted Frank, who contacted Donald, who subsequently contacted the Trump National Guard to protect us.

But I had known nothing about any of the drama until now. Later that day NBC and the pageant officials asked me if I wanted to continue with the plans to host the telecast that night. The man's whereabouts were still unknown, and it was possible he was already in Atlantic City, perhaps even planning to be there in the convention center when the pageant aired at eight P.M., but definitely still armed and dangerous.

My answer was typical. "Hell, yes," I told them.

You can't let crazy people make *you* crazy. (This was before Beth Chapman.)

Perhaps some felt it was foolish to needlessly endanger myself and my child, but I never gave that a thought. It's like the terrorists today—you're aware that the danger exists, but they are victorious only when we allow them the power to intimidate us and change the way we choose to live our lives.

Plus, I know Donald Trump, and there was no way he was gonna let anything happen to us on his watch.

Well, I stood in the wings listening to the parade of states, absolutely confident that I was doing what I was hired to do, my daughter safe and sound in the Trump Plaza Hotel a few blocks away, surrounded by a large group of very large men who wanted to keep working for Donald Trump for the rest of their lives.

The pageant went on as planned without incident, and frankly, I can't remember who was crowned the new Miss America. I bet you can't, either.

We flew home that night, and when we arrived, I hugged Cody as tightly as I could without breaking him.

The next day I took him to see a movie along with a bodyguard who very much seemed to enjoy *Robin Hood: Men in Tights*.

As we were walking to our car afterward, the bodyguard received a call.

"It's over, Mrs. Gifford," he told me, returning his phone to its place right near his gun. "We got the bastard."

Oh, yeah, now I remember who won: the good guys.

Attitude of Gratitude

I don't understand when this attitude of entitlement entered our nation's consciousness.

I seem to recall a pretty good speech by John F. Kennedy a few years back admonishing us to "Ask not what your country can do for you. Ask what you can do for your country."

Well, that concept went out with the hula hoop, honey.

Now it's "Where's mine? And how soon do I get it?"

The Greatest Generation has been replaced by a younger In-Gratest Generation, and I think our nation's founders would all turn over in their respective graves and grit their collective wooden teeth in despair if they could see it.

Now we live in a culture where parents want to be their children's best friends more than they want to be their children's best parents. And they think their children need *things* far more than they need *them*.

So as a result we have a generation of designer-clad, iPod-ed, iPhoned, and PC-ed kids who hate their parents with all their hip and hardened hearts.

As Dr. Phil would say, "So, how's that workin' for ya?"

P.S. I remember when my daddy was offered a lucrative new job years ago.

"Will it take me away from my family?" he asked his prospective boss.

"Well, yes," the prospective boss answered.

"Then, no, but thank you kindly," my daddy responded. "I think my kids need their daddy more than they need a new TV."

P.P.S. I still need my daddy.

Technically Happy

I AM PROBABLY THE MOST TECHNOLOGY CHALLENGED PERSON YOU will ever meet. I don't know how to turn on a computer. I don't email or instant message.

I do, however, congratulate myself when I actually fax something successfully. My iPod has been plugged into the outlet pretty much since Cass and Cody bought me one for my birthday. My fiftieth, I think.

I just got a cell phone about a year ago. That, I'm proud to say, I actually handle very well. Unless I have to email or instant message, of course. I also write all my musicals, screenplays, books, and songs by hand on yellow legal pads with my Z4 Roller Bic pens. Perhaps upon reading this you find yourself thinking "Boy, that Kathie Lee is an idiot."

Hey, I've been called worse.

But before you pass judgment, ponder this:

I might just be a happier person than you are because

1. I don't depend on a computer that crashes and gets viruses. (Or is it a fungus? See I don't give a rip.)
2. I don't have a BlackBerry that suddenly goes dead, taking with it every telephone number and address of everyone I have ever known since the day I was born, which was a very long time ago.
3. I don't come home at the end of the day to 462 emails I don't want to answer.
4. I don't have more spam than my mother could eat in a year.

I'm tech-free.
Now, that may make me an idiot.
But you know what?
It also makes me a happy idiot.

Odd-servations

OKAY, I WAS WRONG THAT FINDING A GRAY HAIR IN MY NOSE meant that the world is coming to an end. But this time I'm not wrong. I have just seen the new commercial Viva Viagra with the guy in the cheesy blue suit wooing his long-suffering wife with hideous fake red roses to dance with him (his idea of fore-play?), and then, when he's obviously incapable of carrying her up the stairs, she gleefully agrees to climb them herself, only to let him triumphantly lift her into his polyester-covered arms and carry her over the threshold into marital bedroom bliss. I actually felt a need to pray for the woman.

What has she done in her life to deserve such a punish-ment? I mean, for that suit alone he should be put away. For a very long time. Much longer than his four-hour erection.

Here's the thing: You need look no further than the advertisements on TV to understand that CIVILIZATION AS WE HAVE KNOWN IT IS *OVER*.

You want to lose ten pounds real fast? All you have to do is take a little pill. Course, then you might also get a bad case of anal leakage. But what's a little greasy discharge among skinny friends? No pain, no gain. Or in this case, no *loss*. It's crazy. But it's seductive.

Personally, I'm tempted to try that restless leg syndrome medicine just to experience the "uncontrollable sexual urges" it warns about.

I wonder what would happen if you took the restless leg syndrome pill and that weight loss pill at the same time? Would you get an uncontrollable urge to . . . never mind.

And it's amazing to me that some of the biggest stars in the world agree to appear in these embarrassing commercials. Now, I think Sally Field is a brilliant actress, but it's hard to believe she has osteoporosis. Nor do I believe Jamie Lee Curtis has trouble going to the bathroom. I don't think Almay is what gives Reese Witherspoon the strength to get through her day. Nor do I believe for a minute that Robert J. Wagner has a reverse mortgage.

But I do like the idea of Ed McMahon sitting in one of those instant bathtubs with the handlebars. That's a scream.

Oh—and I do believe the little baby doing E*TRADE while projectile vomiting is the cutest thing I've ever seen, except for the one when he hires Bobo, the creepy clown. Absolute genius.

But it's not just commercials. It's the talk shows, too. Today's shows makes me miss Johnny Carson. And Jack Paar. And Merv Griffin, Mike Douglas, and Dick Cavett. I miss people who knew how to talk to people intelligently, without insulting or demeaning them, and also knew how to listen.

And while I'm at it, I miss Bill Cosby, Bob Newhart, Tim Conway, Carol Burnett—people who knew how to make you laugh without making you feel guilty about it.

Sex does not automatically equal entertainment. Filthy words do not automatically make someone a comedian. And screaming and interrupting certainly does not equal having a conversation.

Our culture is so sex-saturated that the media has actually succeeded in making sex boring.

There used to be more to sitcoms, more to movies, music, and books and magazines.

Remember when it was "Two ducks went into a bar . . ."?

Now it's "Two horny ducks with herpes go into a strip club . . ."

Can we please get over our sex organs and get a life?

P.S. My agent just called with a lucrative hemorrhoid ointment offer. I'm tempted. I mean, nobody believes these things, right?

Left Out

I HAVE ALREADY DESCRIBED IN HORRIFIC DETAIL HOW MY BODY IS falling apart. But I neglected to tell you one extremely interesting fact regarding my epidermal disintegration, otherwise and henceforth known as ED.

That's right, I've got a bad case of a different kind of ED, and unfortunately there's no pill for it.

Okay, so here it is: The left side of my entire body has been deteriorating at a far more rapid pace than my right side. I mean dramatically.

Now, I know nobody but Angelina Jolie is perfectly symmetrical, but this borders on the ludicrous and truly pathetic.

First it started with my left eye, which now completely rejects contact lenses of any kind. Then it moved south to the left part of my top lip, which crinkles up as if I've been smoking out of the left side of my mouth since I was twelve.

I would describe to you my left breast, but then I would have to shoot you. (Cody would never nurse on it. Everybody's a critic.)

My left arm has been numb and tingly since I herniated a disk two years ago. Moving south: left thigh? Far more dimpled than the right thigh, which makes no sense because I sit on my fat ass all day long with my booty nicely and evenly distributed, thank you for asking.

And then my left knee is markedly more gnarly than the other one even though I'm careful to cross them alternately.

And finally, the aforementioned feet.

The left bunion was twice as big as the right one, and the next toe was completely dislocated thanks to the evil genius Rupert Holmes and his torturous play, *Thumbs.*

Oh, speaking of *Thumbs,* that reminds me of my hands, which I *left* out.

I already told you how Cody broke my ring finger, remember? Well, yeah, *of course,* the ring finger is on your *left* hand.

So there you have it.

You probably don't give a royal rip unless you have noticed such an unusual shift in your own personal ED as well, and in that case "you're welcome."

I draw no conclusions—political, religious, or otherwise— regarding this phenomenon.

But I've got to stop writing for a while because I suddenly have a spasm in my left foot where my worst bunion used to be.

So now you're thinking that I'm not only an idiot, but I'm a freak, too, right?

Right.

I couldn't agree with you more.

P.S. I have just been diagnosed with BURSITIS in my—yes, you guessed it!—LEFT shoulder.

It Suits You Fine

You know how great it feels to finally clean out some of those long forgotten drawers we all have?

Well, sometimes it backfires on you, too. Like the other day . . .

I was rummaging through one such drawer when suddenly I came upon some bathing suits I had long ago saved, thinking that someday I would lose enough weight to wear them again.

I don't know what I was smoking that day, because I swear to God these bathing suits looked like the kind that little girls dress their dolls in.

Cassidy could put them on her Barbies, if she still played with them. But she is too old for that now. How could so much time have gone by so quickly, and how could the pounds have crept up on me in the meantime?

I truly believe those bikinis would be too small for even Cassidy to wear, and she happens to be a size zero. Geez.

So after I got over the shock, I remembered a story Joanie had told me a few years before. At the time I thought it was cute. Now I find it pathetically true and almost unbearably sad.

It seems that it was time for Mom to buy a new bathing suit. She loved to swim, but she had put off buying a new bathing suit for way too long and could no longer be seen in the one she had. So she went to a nice store in Rehoboth Beach and asked a very pleasant saleslady to help her.

Together they picked out some in her size, and she headed into the dressing room to try them on.

"How's it going, Mrs. Epstein?" The saleslady asked politely from outside the door.

"Oh, fine," Joanie answered, struggling to arrange her flop bags into the tad-too-small top.

"I think this one is good, but it's hard to tell in here."

By now Joanie could hear two teenagers trying on suits in the stall next to hers.

"Come on out," the saleslady coaxed. "There's a much better mirror out here."

Reluctantly, Joanie emerged and stood before the full-length mirror in all her body beautiful.

"It looks lovely on you," the saleslady said sincerely, and Joanie was relieved that she had found something flattering.

Suddenly the two teenagers emerged in the tiniest bikinis my mother had ever seen.

They giggled and turned and modeled those postage stamps like they were posing for the *Sports Illustrated* swimsuit issue.

Their bodies were toned and tanned, and they were absolutely adorable.

The saleslady noticed the crestfallen expression on Joanie's face and suddenly took her hand. "Oh, honey," she said sweetly, patting it, "don't worry about it. We had our turn, didn't we?"

Joanie laughed and immediately felt better.

I hope you do, too.

I don't. I feel like crap and I want another turn.

I DO NOT UNDERSTAND the
appeal of thongs.

I mean, why would you want to floss your
heinie?

Life's a Beach

THE LAST TIME I WORE A BATHING SUIT IN PUBLIC WAS TWO
Christmases ago. We were on a friend's charter boat in the Vir-
gin Islands and everyone wanted to go to the Soggy Dollar Bar
on Jost Van Dyke island, which, unfortunately, you have to
swim to.

I looked out to the island from the aft of the boat, and my
heart sank. There must have been a hundred people already
there, and some of them were already eating that delicious jerk
chicken that the islands are known for. I could smell it wafting
in the breeze, and it made me crazy.

My stomach began to gurgle, so I plunged into the water
and burnt a couple of calories swimming to the shore—maybe
enough to counteract the parsley garnish. The minute I got
there, I took a beach towel and wrapped my butt up like a

sausage, and I never took it off until it was time to swim back after lunch.

There were many, many people on that beach who were, shall we say, "bodaciously challenged." There were boobies as big as watermelons, guts as big as tires, and butts as big as the *Hindenburg* everywhere you looked. There were also thighs that defied description, and I bet they came with a bad case of chappedness.

But no one seemed to care.

Oh, how I envied those people! I can't imagine what life would be like with that kind of "who gives a rip" self-image.

But maybe it's because they know that their pictures are never going to end up in one of those tabloids with the caption: "What the hell happened to Kathie Lee's ass?"

Or the E! channel's wonderful and extremely educational new special, *30 Best and Worst Beach Bodies,* where they magnify the cellulite on your leg so much that it looks like a slab of Swiss cheese gone bad.

Lately I won't even wear a bathing suit at my own pool in my own backyard.

Why? BECAUSE THEY HAVE SPY SATELLITES IN THE SKY that can beam down a signal from a thousand miles away and catch you doing private things that should remain private for the sake of civilization.

That's why.

Howls and Bowels

FRANK HAS BEEN FRIENDS SINCE THE THIRD GRADE WITH A GENTLE-man from Bakersfield, California, named Bob Karpe. Frank loves to reminisce and tell us stories of their fishing and foot-ball adventures when they were teenagers.

Well, it's been more than sixty years since they were teenagers, but they still visit each other once or twice a year.

I love that about Frank. He really does treasure the people who have been with him pretty much all his life.

When Cassidy was six, Bob came to visit us at our summer house in Nantucket. The years have been kind to Bob finan-cially, but they've taken quite a toll on him physically, and he had a long, difficult trip to this little island thirty miles off the Cape Cod coast.

Bob pretty much disappeared into our guest room for the first two days. He came downstairs only to occasionally join us for a meal, smoke a cigar, and then head up the stairs again to rest and take Senokot. Cassidy found this strange, but we told her he was having a little digestion trouble and was battling a bad case of constipation.

One night around the dinner table we decided to ask each person what they thought was the key to happiness.

Frank said something about family, Cody said something about sports, probably. And so around the table we went.

I said how much faith means in a person's life. Bob gave quite a lengthy dissertation about friendship.

Finally it was Cassidy's turn.

"Cass," I asked, "what do you think is the most important thing in life, honey? The key to happiness?"

She didn't hesitate for a second.

"Pooing."

Bob Karpe, who hadn't been able to poo for three days, suddenly changed his mind.

"She's right," he boomed. "Family, friends, and football don't mean a damn thing if you can't poop."

All of a sudden Bob started laughing so hard the bowels of the earth literally "moved" beneath him.

Cass was very pleased with herself.

Bob Karpe was a new man.

Frank with Bob Karpe in Nantucket, right after the earth moved. No wonder he's smiling.

This Means War

Frank is off in the next room watching Oliver North's *War Stories*.

I have learned through experience that I cannot compete with any war. Not even the Falklands War, not even the Battle of the Frickin Bulge. They were all too powerful, too exciting, and way, way too thrilling for me to expect to be relevant in any way.

Maybe if I put on a uniform, wave a flag, or drop a bomb on him, he'll notice?

Nope. Sometimes I think he'll only look up if I gain so much weight that I start to resemble a battleship.

That'll teach him.

I'm Feeling Peevish

EVERYBODY HAS THEIR OWN UNIQUE SET OF PET PEEVES. THINGS that, though relatively insignificant when compared to, say, a terrorist nuclear attack, are still able to drive a person absolutely bonkers.

Now, a pet peeve has virtually nothing to do with an actual pet—unless, of course, one of your pet peeves is people who don't pick up their pet's poo-poo in public places.

I have friends who believe that people who do this should be dung—sorry, hung. Or if the death penalty does not apply in that state, at least forced to live inside a five-by-five cell with a couple of Saint Bernards with diarrhea for the rest of their miserable lives.

I, of course, am a much nicer person, and my pet peeves are just a tad more benign. They are as follows, and in no particular order (it really depends on the day):

1. People who scream into cell phones, completely oblivious to their surroundings
2. People who butt in any kind of line
3. People who charge out of elevators with absolutely no concern for people actually trying to get in them, OR vice versa
4. People who are incapable of saying "please" and "thank you"
5. People who pick their noses in public
6. People who then think nothing of eating whatever it is they just picked
7. People who talk during movies or plays or church or, most important, one of my songs
8. People who munch so loudly that Dolby Surround Sound cannot drown them out
9. People who park their pickup trucks, cars, RVs, boats, and motorcycles on their grass
10. People who leave children's toys out in their yards all year long, even when their children never play with them or have long since gone off to college, graduated, and had children of their own who also never play with them
11. People who never even try to pick up a tab—it would break their arm
12. People who do not discipline their children when they throw over-the-top-beyond-belief-in-your-face-out-of-control temper tantrums
13. People who do not use napkins
14. People who do not flush toilets
15. People who do not wash their hands after they have not used their napkins and then gone to the bathroom without flushing the toilet

I'm sure there are a few more, but I'm exhausted due to my peevishness.

P.S. I just remembered one more: people who eat like pigs without using a napkin, who then go to the bathroom without flushing the toilet or washing their hands, who then shake mine, which I just washed after eating politely and using my napkin.

DON'T YOU HATE IT when people say, "Oh, you look so tired."

They try to make it sound like they're concerned for you, but the truth is they're secretly thrilled you look worse than the last time they saw you.

It's like when a particular Southern lady I know said, "Oh, poor Peggy Sue. She's gained two hundred pounds, bless her heart."

Right. "Bless her big fat lard-ass heart" is what she really means.

Not nice. But let's forgive her.

She's probably tired.

Wordy

I love words. (Most of them, anyway.)

Certain words make me smile. I like to say them over and over because they feel good in my mouth. It's fun, try it.

Say "goiter." See? Goiters make you giggle. Unless you have one.

The other day Frank and I were talking about some playboy kind of guy who was in the news at the time—a real player.

"I guess he's cut quite a swath," I said.

"Quite a swath," Frank agreed.

That's when I decided that "swath" is one of my new favorite words and I can't wait to try it out in all kinds of sentences I've never used before.

"Cody, I better not catch you cutting a swath at school."

Or "How was your weekend, Hoda? Did you cut a swath?"

All right, so it doesn't always work.

Joanie loves to say "smitten." I think it's because it has a sort of biblical ring to it: David was smitten with Bathsheba so he went and had her husband, Uriah the Hittite, smote.

But I think my favorite is "umbrage," as in "Donald Trump took umbrage when the reporter asked him about his hair." You wonder what exactly umbrage is and where does one actually take it when one actually has it?

See what I mean? Words are fun.

I'm smitten with them.

No Offense

WHAT'S ABSOLUTELY CERTAIN ABOUT LIVE TV IS THAT YOU ARE bound to offend someone on a daily basis. Even if you have absolutely no ill will toward anyone, no ax to grind, no hidden agenda, and not one ounce of malice in your DNA, you can bet your baby's butt that somebody is going to take umbrage at something that you say during the course of an hour show.

I can't imagine why, but apparently I say things that upset people far more than Hoda does.

So, I suggested to Brian Balthazar, our producer, a solution to all the ruckus I seem to inspire.

"Brian," I said, "just get rid of that NBC News logo that's always scrawling across the bottom of the screen."

"And . . . ?" He looked at me suspiciously because he knows me now.

"And just put up one that says, 'Kathie Lee Gifford would like to apologize for what she just said, what she is presently saying, and what she is bound to say any second now.'"

He was considering it when he quit.

What's in a Name?

PEOPLE ARE SO FUNNY. THEY GET ABSOLUTELY FLUMMOXED WHEN they meet someone famous. Often they will say, "Oh my God! You're my biggest fan!" when, of course, that's ridiculous because you've never even met them before.

Or they'll say: "I know you! You're . . . You're . . . Who are you again?"

And then you'll say your own name as graciously as possible, and they'll say, "No, you're not." Or "No—I *hate* her!"

I try not to take any of it personally, but sometimes you want to wet your pants it's so funny.

Once Frank was going through security at LaGuardia Airport. One of the people on duty recognized him instantly and blurted, "I know you! I know you! You . . . You . . . You married to Regis!"

Frank just said "That's right" and kept going.

Even Hoda admitted to me recently that she goes to the same bodega every morning to get her newspaper. The man always smiles and says, "I love you, Kathie Lee." For months she tried to explain to him that her name is Hoda and she is Kathie Lee's co-host on the fourth hour of *Today*. He would just smile and nod and say, "I know. I know. I love you, Kathie Lee."

Finally she just gave up.

Now she says "I love you, too" and keeps going.

I too have my own flummoxed celebrity encounter moments.

The other day I was waiting for a friend for lunch at Michael's restaurant, when the head of CBS, Les Moonves, arrived with his lunch guest.

I said a quick hello to Les and turned as his friend followed him to their table.

"Hi." I smiled, extending my hand. "Kathie Gifford."

"Hi," he said, and smiled back. "Robert Altman."

Suddenly a light went off.

"Oh, of course," I said. "I'm a huge fan of your work."

He twitched just a tad, but I thought nothing of it.

Until a moment later when I realized that Robert Altman, the famous director, whose work I was so fond of, was DEAD. And had been for a long time.

This Robert Altman seated next to me was a lawyer from Washington, D.C., married to Lynda Carter, who used to be Wonder Woman.

Check, please.

P.S. I still feel like an idiot.

The Welcome Matt

It took about three and a half months to get Matt Lauer to our house for dinner. This is a man who has to check his calendar to see if he'll be in Afghanistan or Machu Picchu or China hosting the Olympics, or in Iran interviewing that party animal Ahmadinejad.

You never know where in the world the guy might be, so I was delighted when we finally picked a Tuesday night late in July that worked for him.

I had checked with all our colleagues at the *Today* show about what to serve. Everybody said the same thing: "He'll eat anything."

I found that hard to believe. Matt is in unbelievable shape. I couldn't picture him wolfing down a sizzling fat T-bone steak with an ice cream chaser.

But, because of the responses I got from his co-workers and his assistant, Jackie, that's exactly what we served.

He came bearing gifts. Just like Billy Joel: "A bottle of red, a bottle of white."

Well, as the evening progressed, it just got more and more like it was being filmed for a Hollywood movie. We sat out by Precious, the aforementioned pig, and began to dine on Frank's delicious steak, mashed potatoes, salad, mozzarella and tomatoes, and broccoli.

All of a sudden two geese (we call them Moishe and Golda) swam by. Rabbits followed.

Matt accused me of pressing some button that had cued them. Then seagulls flew by, squawking a welcome. He accused me again. Then sailboats with sails aflutter regatta-ed by in rhythm. And finally, as the full moon began to rise, a *stealth bomber* suddenly appeared above us.

A stealth bomber!

Frank and I had never seen such a phenomenon. But Matt didn't believe us.

Regardless, there it was. Undeniable. Extraordinary against the perfect summer sky.

Matt later sent us a thank-you note, wondering if our unicorn had been busy at a children's party.

No, I'd had it tied up in the garage. I'd just thought it would be a bit much for a guy like Matt who doesn't get out much.

Jerusalem Rocks!

I ADORE ISRAEL. ITALY AND ISRAEL ARE MY TWO FAVORITE PLACES IN the world besides my own backyard. In Italy you get better food, but Israel wins big-time when it comes to the impact it's had on history.

The first time I visited was in 1971. I was graduating from high school and I couldn't wait to see the promised land. My parents had given me a trip to Israel to attend the Jerusalem Conference on Biblical Prophecy. I've never been able to get enough of this stuff, and the moment my mom and I walked off the EL AL airplane in Tel Aviv, I was home. I missed my high school graduation ceremony, but I couldn't have cared less. I was in the cradle of civilization, baby!

Several years later I was hired to perform in a documentary a producer was shooting, and so once again I made the trip to the Holy Land.

I really think to get anywhere close to understanding all its mysteries, you'd need to spend years there to sift through all the artifacts, and examine all the caves, and visit all the archaeological digs unearthing fresh discoveries every day.

Israel boggles the brain while it satisfies the soul. I couldn't wait to share it with my sister. A couple of years later we traveled together to Israel to tape a television special.

Most of our time was spent singing musical numbers at the many well-known biblical sites. But we always tried to save a little time just to explore some of the local color on our own.

One day, after taping in the Old City, we decided to walk home, down the mountain, into the Kidron Valley and then up through the Mount of Olives back to our hotel. It was an amazingly beautiful afternoon with the waning angle of the sun, the birds chirping, and not a soul in sight.

We felt like we were in a scene right out of a Cecil B. De-Mille movie. I seriously expected Charlton Heston to show up in his skirt and ask "How ya doin', ladies?"

Just as we were reaching the valley, we looked up toward the Golden Gate, and there was an unbelievable sight. Several shepherds dressed in traditional ancient garb were guarding their flock of sheep.

We couldn't believe it! Instantly we grabbed our cameras and took as many pictures as we could. Then we continued on, talking excitedly about how fortunate we were to have stumbled on such an incredible scene at exactly the right time.

All of a sudden we could hear stones rolling down the hill and could feel them landing at our feet. Several of them hit the backs of our legs. And then much bigger rocks started hurling toward us. We looked up, and the once genteel shepherds were now running at us, waving their staffs in the air, and shouting something in Arabic that instinctively I was pretty sure was not friendly in nature. As tired as we were, we hustled our butts up to the Mount of Olives faster than you can say "Holy Moses."

It turns out that we had committed an unforgivable sin: We had taken the shepherds' pictures without paying for them. Can you imagine? I wonder if they would have taken my American Express card.

Eventually they gave up and returned to their flock, and Michie and I went home with an unbelievable memory and the pictures to prove it.

How many people can say they got stoned in Jerusalem and lived to tell about it?

P.S. I'm sitting in my backyard right now, and it looks pretty damned good to me. I'm pretending Frank is Charlton Heston and he's got his staff and . . .

PEOPLE HAVE BEEN SO NICE

to me since I came back to television full-time.
I can't tell you how good it feels to know that
our show is touching people and hopefully
giving them a giggle before they get on with
their busy day.

One lady came up to me last summer in
Nantucket and said, "I love seeing you on the
Today show. I've missed you since you left
TV. I used to watch you all the time and I've
read all your books."

"Thank you so much," I said, and smiled.
"Well, then you'll be glad to know I'm writing a
new book right now that'll be out next spring."

"Great!" she replied. "Just don't put too
much God in it."

"I'll pray about it," I laughed.

Pass the Bread

WE'VE TRIED TO TAKE THE KIDS TO CHURCH EVERY WEEK SINCE they were born, but it's been a battle most Sundays. It wasn't until a few years ago that we found a great church with great music, and all of a sudden it was actually fun to go to church together as a family.

One time we were attending a Sunday morning service at a small church we were visiting in Florida. The pastor started the Communion ritual. It was the first time Cass had seen the bread and wine, and she blurted out, "Look, Cody! This church serves *snacks*!"

I hope somewhere in heaven Jesus laughed, 'cause I sure did.

P.S. I have searched the Bible on this one. I did find a scripture that said "Jesus wept," but I'm still looking for "Jesus laughed." I'm sure I'll find it, because those disciples were real party animals.

Mercy Me

THIS MAY SURPRISE YOU, BUT I'M NOT A BIG FAN OF RELIGION. I think more damage has been done and more evil perpetrated on the planet "in the name of God" than because of any other single destructive force.

Personally, I am not interested in following a god that requires me to blow up myself or anybody else.

Maybe I'm a little old-fashioned. I like the idea of God as an all-knowing, all-powerful, and yet all-MERCIFUL being—one that loves me enough to forgive all my stupidity and selfishness and arrogance. Oh, did I mention ignorance? No? Okay, my ignorance, too.

Now, I'm not talking about the way-out-there, mumbo jumbo, you channel me, I'll channel you, kumbaya, touchy-feely fluff stuff.

No. I mean love, L-O-V-E.

But that's the problem. The English language has only one word for love, and love means different things to different people (just ask Joey Buttafuoco). But those Greeks—they were smart. They had three different words for love:

1. Eros: meaning erotic, sexual love (which ain't bad)
2. Philadelphia—meaning brotherly love (which is a good idea, too), and
3. Agape: meaning divine, unconditional love—the kind a creator has for his creation

The closest I've ever come to agape love is with my children, but even with them there have been times when I've wanted to destroy what I had created. Thank God that feeling didn't last long.

But my *spouse?* Show me one married person who has unconditional love for their husband or wife. That's why they call it a marriage *contract.* Because there are a whole lot of conditions. And then there are certain friends who have fallen off the friend list, haven't they? And they know why.

So that leaves agape love, which, in my heart of hearts, is what I know I have on a deeper level, or a higher plane, in a different dimension, than any other kind of love I have ever known.

And I can't imagine having to get through a day without it—what with kids, and marriage, and hot flashes, and flop bags, and critics, and Beth Chapman and all.

Blame It on Aimee

MANY GOOD THINGS HAPPEN TO YOU BY DEFAULT. AFTER I LEFT *Live,* I started writing songs with a vengeance. With time on my hands for the first time in my life, I felt like the little boy with his finger in the dam. Once that finger was gone, the creative floodgates were open. Once *Live* was over, it was, "Bring it on, baby, and let's see where this big river flows."

So, I was sitting in our sunroom in Nantucket writing throughout that first work-free summer, when the phone rang. It was Jimmy Nederlander, the famed Broadway producer responsible for more Tony awards than anyone else in history.

"I want you to do *Mame* for me," he said in his distinctive, lovable way. "I think you look too young to be Mame, but what do you think?"

"I think I look old enough to play Mame's mother," I answered honestly. "You haven't seen me in a while."

Jimmy chuckled at that.

"But I can't, Jimmy. My daddy's really sick and I can't commit to anything long-term, especially out of town."

Jimmy considered this for a moment.

"Well, how am I gonna get you to work with me?" he persisted.

"Well," I suggested, "I'm working on something right now you might be interested in."

I went on to tell him about the musical I had begun working on with my two composer friends, David Pomeranz and David Friedman, about the famed female evangelist, Aimee Semple McPherson. In the 1920s and 1930s she had been the most controversial, most celebrated figure in the country. "I'm old enough to remember her," Jimmy said excitedly. "She was quite a broad."

Jimmy remembered right. Aimee had been married three times, divorced twice, had been the defendant in the trial of the century for corruption of morals and obstruction of justice, and had ultimately died of an accidental overdose of barbiturates. But she also saved one and a half million people from starving to death and built a temple in Los Angeles that is still vibrant today, caring for thirty thousand of the worst of the down and out in the worst neighborhood in the city every day of the year.

Eventually Jimmy asked a question that changed my life.

"When do I get to hear the music?"

"As soon as I can record the songs!" I answered, trying not to sound too eager. "I'll bring a CD to your office and play them for you." Nine months later, I did.

I played five songs for Jimmy and his wife, Charlene. It only took about twenty minutes, but it seemed like an eternity.

Jimmy kept looking down at the conference table, drumming his fingers on it while he listened. After each song he'd lift his head, cock it to the side, and look at me quizzically. He'd then repeat this behavior during the next number.

Oy!

Finally the last song ended and a very uncomfortable silence filled the room.

"I hate everything," Jimmy declared. "Don't I, Charlene?"

Charlene, his beautiful, sophisticated producing partner wife, agreed. "He hates everything," she said, nodding her head.

"But *this* I *love!*" he declared. "Let's do it." I thought I had died and gone straight to heaven. To say I was stunned is a complete and utter understatement. It turns out that each time he had looked up, Jimmy had actually been thinking, "*You wrote this?*"

I gathered up the CD player and my sheet music, and just as I was about to leave, Jimmy said one more thing that completely threw me for a loop: "When do I get to see the book?" he asked, referring to the script.

Damn! The *book!* I knew I'd forgotten something.

"Uh-uh..." I stuttered. "Yeah, the book...Uh...Right..." I did some fast mental calculations.

"Let's see," I thought, "it's right before Memorial Day. I'll get some schmuck to write the book—how hard could it be?"

"And I'll have it for you right after Labor Day," I announced confidently. "No problem."

"All right," Jimmy said, walking back to his office. "Have it on my desk the day after Labor Day."

Well, I left the Nederlander office that day as euphoric as I have ever felt. As soon as I got into the car, I called my daddy with the unbelievable news.

"Daddy!" I literally yelled into the car phone. "Remember

all those years ago when you told me to learn to make my own music?"

My daddy struggled to respond.

"It's going to Broadway!" I joyfully exclaimed. "Broadway, Daddy!"

I could hear his gurgled, excited reaction. It broke my heart he couldn't say the words I knew he was trying to. But it didn't matter, really. I could hear his heart.

True to my word, that book was on Jimmy's desk by Labor Day, but it took a long, circuitous trip getting there.

First I called my dear friend Rupert Holmes, who is the only person who has ever won the Tony for Best Score, Best Book, and Best Musical for his brilliant, *The Mystery of Edwin Drood.* We had become close when I'd performed in one of his hysterical plays, *Thumbs,* at the Helen Hayes Theater.

Rupert's a genius, and everybody knows it. But he's also the sweetest man I've ever met in the theater world.

Rupert delivered about ten pages, but they didn't capture the essence of the story, and he knew it.

"*You* have to write it, Kath," he told me matter-of-factly. "You are the one with the passion for Aimee and all the knowledge. You know her better than anyone."

He was right about the passion part. I had been fascinated by this extraordinary woman for more than twenty-five years.

"Give it a try, sweetheart," Rupert encouraged me. "And I'll help you every step of the way."

I worked all summer long trying to synthesize Aimee's epic life down to two acts.

By the time my effort arrived on Jimmy Nederlander's desk, it was epic all right: two hundred pages and four hours long epic.

After an arduous reading with the Tony-winning actress Christine Ebersole as Aimee, Jimmy made his opinion known.

"I still like the music," he said, "but the book stinks. Fix the book and we'll talk."

Well, it's eight years and a hundred rewrites later and I'm still fixing the book. We've had endless readings, a full workshop in White Plains, New York, and an extremely well-received full production in Washington, D.C., in the spring of 2007 with the extraordinary two-time Tony-nominated actress Carolee Carmello.

In my opinion, having Carolee is like having Barbra Streisand as a singer and Meryl Streep as an actress all rolled into one. I honestly believe she is the finest actress working in the musical theater today, and I'm not alone. She just hasn't had her role of a lifetime yet.

We're both hoping that Aimee is that role. Now all we need is a theater on Broadway before we both get too old to actually do it.

The problem is getting the right director, the right producer, the right theater, and the necessary money all at the same time.

Jimmy and I ultimately parted ways due to creative differences, but that doesn't mean we won't come to some kind of an agreement again.

He started me on one of the most surprising journeys of my life, but it's a more complicated trip than I had ever imagined and a far more difficult process than I can begin to even describe.

Basically, if anyone had told me ten years ago that writing a musical is the *easy* part, I would have called them crazy. But unfortunately, they're right. As hard as it is, it is the easy part.

Hey, at least I've come this far. And it ain't over yet. I just saw Jimmy the other night at a cocktail party.

"How's *Aimee* coming?" he asked me, genuinely interested.

"It's coming, Jimmy," I answered with all the confidence I truly do feel. "It's coming."

P.S. If any of you are interested in investing twelve million dollars in a fantastic Broadway musical, please call me.

The Sign

On a blustery, wet, bitter morning in November 2002 I stepped out onto the patio knowing that this day was going to be one of the most difficult days I would ever have to face. My daddy was to leave the hospital in Rehoboth Beach, Delaware, to be taken home for hospice care. There would be no more attempts to prolong his life.

I had been going back and forth visiting him, of course, but this had such a finality to it.

This trip would be the last time I would ever see my father alive. The last time I would ever smell the Old Spice on his sweet neck. The last time I would ever hold his beautiful hands in mine, and the last time I would kiss him goodbye.

Even now, more than six years later, I have to battle tears, remembering.

Standing there with the rain in my face, I prayed for strength. But, selfishly, I prayed for even more.

"Please, Lord," I whispered into the wind, "please give me a sign that I'll always have my daddy."

At that very moment I looked up into the huge, majestic oak tree that has stood in that yard for more than a hundred years. It's always been my favorite tree, situated right there where so much of our family life takes place. Its branches always seemed to reach out forever, as if trying to embrace the whole world.

Suddenly I saw it.

One leaf—the very last one—was clinging to its branch with all its might. It was so valiant, so brave and determined to stay where it had been for so long.

Cynics, of course, will tell you these things happen by coincidence, and perhaps, for them, they do. Who am I to say? But no one will ever be able to convince me that this was not the very sign I had just prayed for.

And it was saying, "He is with you. He is battling for his life and soon he will let go. But just as sure as spring you will see him again."

I went into our sunroom and wrote these words, so moved by the experience I had just been privileged to share.

HE IS WITH YOU

Old Man winter is creeping up the hill
I can hear his icy fingers tapping on the windowsill
I can see his frosty footsteps as he whistles thru the weeds
And the little squirrel hurries to gather what he needs

Old Mother Nature is dressing in her cloak
As the last leaf dances on the branches of the oak
It's time to draw the curtains as the fall draws to a close
And listen to the secret only Mother Nature knows

He is with you
All who've come before and gone, go on here with you
As a new dawn breaks, new life awakes within you
As sure as every flower reaches to the sun
He is with you
Unseen by human eyes he breathes the air
And whispers up a prayer
That you will hear his sighs
And you will realize
He's there

In the glowing embers, in the frozen riverbed
Mother Nature dreams her summer dreams as snow falls
    overhead
The rose is only sleeping, and soon, before too long
The daffodil will waken to the sparrow's tender song

He is with you
All who've come before and gone, go on here with you
Though they seem to disappear
They're here, still with you
Sure as every mountain reaches to the sky
He is with you

He is reaching out his arms to hold you near
Year after lonely year
And he will never leave
As long as you believe he's here
No, you'll never have to grieve

As long as you believe
He's here
The dogwood only slumbers, and soon she too shall wake
And the swan will swim with her children again on the silent
*   silvery lake.*

At Rehoboth Beach with "Sitting Shiva." Every moment with my daddy was precious.

Building a Bridge

WHEN CASS WAS IN THE THIRD GRADE, PART OF HER HOMEWORK was to read each night for at least thirty minutes. I can't count the number of books we went through.

Some of them were charming, but most, I regret to say, were completely forgettable.

Then one cold autumn night we ran out of books. "Cass," I instructed, "go look in your bookcase. There's got to be a book we haven't read yet."

Dutifully she did what I'd suggested, and after several searches she came back to the sofa carrying a very worn, obviously very old little book.

"Here, Mommy," she said, handing it to me. "Let's read this one."

I'd never seen it before, and I had no idea how it had found its way into our home. I looked at the title, *The Family Under the Bridge.* A sticker on the front proclaimed that it was a winner of the 1959 Newbery Medal for excellence in children's literature.

"Let's try it," I told her, trying to sound enthusiastic. "It's old, but it might be good."

Well, it turned out to be a lot better than good. It was great, and by the time we'd finished this beautiful story of a cranky old Parisian hobo named Armand and the little homeless family he befriends at Christmastime, I was a goner. I was sobbing my eyes out.

Cass loved it, too, and suggested we read it again right away. That had never happened before. So we did, and this time I cried even harder. Cass looked at me and said, "Geez, Mama, get a grip." Afterward I couldn't get it out of my head.

We left to go to Florida for Christmas vacation, and all I could think of were those three little redheaded, freckled children and their dog who needed a home.

By now I had learned to follow where my passion led me, so by the time we arrived home two weeks later, I had already adapted the book into a two-act play and written the lyrics for twenty songs.

A very poignant moment in the play happens at the beginning of Act II. Armand has taken the three homeless children to stay with his friend Mirelli, who happens to be a gypsy, the very kind of woman that the children's mother harbors a tremendous amount of prejudice against. The mother, Madame Calcet, is herself heartbroken over the recent death of her beloved husband and has lost all joy in her penniless existence. But when Mirelli sings "He Is with You," Madame Calcet's prejudice and sorrow disappear.

I called my friend David Pomeranz about the project, and after one reading of the book he was on board as the composer.

There was only one problem, and it was a doozy: I didn't own the rights to it. HarperCollins did. I called my attorney in New York and explained the situation to him.

"Well," he said wisely, "it sounds delightful, but don't do any work on it until I can secure the rights."

"Too late," I confessed. "I already wrote it."

This is why I doubt I will ever again attempt to option any previously published property: It took well over a year and a fricking fortune to secure the theatrical rights to *The Family Under the Bridge.*

The publisher acted like they had *Harry Potter,* and I pray to God that someday they're right.

Under the Bridge opened off-Broadway for three months in 2004. *The Wall Street Journal* loved it. *The New York Times* hated it. Actually, they hated me and really reviewed my tabloid life instead of the play.

It didn't matter.

It was a glorious, thrilling journey from the first time I read the book with Cassidy to the closing night off-Broadway at the Zipper Theater.

Samuel French published it, and it's now produced in regional theaters all across the country, usually at Christmastime.

It's also in development hell as a feature film starring—I wish I could tell you but then I'd have to have you destroyed.

There's no guarantee it will ever actually come to a theater near you.

But this fat lady hasn't sung yet.

She's just warming up.

Plan Z

Right now I'm looking down on Nantucket Harbor. Well, actually, I'm looking in the direction that I know Nantucket Harbor to be. It sure was there last night.

But, as they say on this island, "Fog happens."

People who live on islands have learned to accept it as a way of life. It's almost a fatalistic attitude, and it serves them well because they always seem to have a Plan B.

I'm all for Plan B's, even C's and D's. I think that's why God made the alphabet. So that every time something goes askew in our lives, we can always make a new plan, twenty-six times if we have to.

This is mentally healthy stuff.

As opposed to the guy I just saw at the airport this morning, screaming at the US Airways representative that they'd better do something about the fog because he wasn't about to sit still with this inconvenience. I'm sure the guy had no idea what a jerk he looked like. People who box with the wind look very stupid.

We had gone to the airport to see Cassidy's friend Boo Boo off to attend a funeral. So you might say she had a darn good reason to scream at someone, too. I mean, funerals don't generally wait for the fog to clear. But the contrast between the man yelling and Boo Boo could not have been more apparent.

The man was frantic. Boo Boo was calm.

The man was fuming. Boo Boo chewed her gum.

When it was finally announced that the flight was canceled, the man went ballistic.

I looked at Boo Boo and said something brilliant like, "Sorry, honey. Fog happens."

So Cass and Boo Boo returned home, delighted that nature had intervened, allowing them to spend some more time together watching one of their favorite Jack Nicholson videos: *Anger Management.*

What So Proudly We Hailed

CASSIDY IS ALMOST SIXTEEN NOW, BUT SHE STILL LOVES TO COMPETE in all the kids' Fourth of July contests in Nantucket. Part of me is thrilled that she's still a little girl and obviously in no rush to grow up. But, I've got to admit, it's starting to get a little weird.

"How long is she going to do this?" Frank asked last Independence Day as we made our way through the crowd of families and strollers and dogs along the cobblestones on Main Street.

"You got me," I answered wisely.

He just rolled his eyes. Frank does that a lot. Anyway, we got to the first competition—the pie-eating contest. For the previous three years Cass had won this one, hands down. And I mean literally hands down because you're not allowed to use your hands. You have to bend over the blueberry pie with your arms clasped behind you and then proceed to stuff the entire pie into your face in the shortest amount of time possible.

She always looks so small to me compared to the other kids in her age group, but let me tell you, once that contest starts, size no longer matters. It's speed, baby, and a certain "Let 'er rip" attitude that apparently Cassidy has inherited from someone who shall remain nameless.

Wham! Within seconds they were handing that blue ribbon to her for the fourth consecutive year.

The people around us could not believe their eyes.

"How does she *do* that?" they asked in amazement.

"That's how she eats at home," I said, and shrugged.

"Wow," they responded.

"Yeah," I said. "Wait till you see what she does to the watermelon."

She didn't disappoint.

Frank just rolled his eyes.

I think he's afraid of what she's going to do to her wedding cake.

The Fun Factor

BEFORE *LIVE WITH REGIS AND KATHIE LEE* WAS SYNDICATED nationally, Regis and I hosted a local New York program called *The Morning Show* for three years. We had a lot of time to get to know each other and to develop the kind of show that really worked for our two personalities. But when Hoda and I first started working together on the fourth hour of the *Today* show, we had never even seen the stools we were going to sit on, never been on the Plaza together, and never done one rehearsal, sound check, or run-through. I think we did a quick lighting check (we're not stupid), but that was it.

We just sat down and did a show. And miraculously, it worked.

Chemistry is something you can count on in a test tube, but let me tell you, it doesn't automatically happen on the boob

Halloween with Regis. The first time we appeared as each other. Even as a man I'm prettier than he is. Now do you see why I'm so obsessed with plucking?

tube. People used to ask Regis and me the secret to our "chemistry."

"It's simple," I always answered. "We have fun."

And it's true, fun is contagious. I have learned this through more than forty years of live performing: If I'm having a good time, the chances are very good that the audience is, too.

So Hoda and I agreed to have the best time together that two women could possibly have for one hour Monday through Friday at ten o'clock in the morning.

I had absolutely no idea if the fun we had at lunch would translate on television, but it was worth a try.

Honestly, I am happy to report that I have been stunned by the success of it. Very few people are blessed to find that kind of chemistry once in life. But twice? And after an eight-year absence?

Unheard of.

Do I think it will last for fifteen years like *Live with Regis and Kathie Lee* did? Absolutely not.

But only because I'm way too old.

I don't want to do the *Today* show in a walker and orthopedic shoes, and I'm sure Hoda has no desire to wipe my drool or change my Depends. But there is hope it will continue nonetheless.

Because someday even Regis Philbin will hang up his microphone, and Kelly Ripa will be looking for a job.

Live Today with Kelly and Hoda Lee.

Now, *that* I want to live long enough to see.

IS IT JUST ME, or is everybody on TV yelling? And worse, they're all yelling at the same time.

And everybody's so angry. Or they're angry that you're not angry about the same thing they're angry about. So they yell louder. Which makes me very, very angry.

Zen Again

I'M A TCHOTCHKE KIND OF GAL. I LIKE KNICKKNACKS AND OB-
jets d'art and lots of clutter. *Organized* clutter. But if one little tchotchke is a mere smidge out of place or at the wrong
angle or too high or too low, watch out. Mama goes a bit
mental.

Suffice it to say I am not what you would call a minimalist.
What's the fun of that when you can be a MAXIMALIST and
drive everyone around you crazy?

Frank swears it takes longer to take the pillows off our bed
than it does to actually sleep in it. He may be right.

He also thinks that guests should not have to remove five
pillows off a couch before they can actually sit on it. He may
have a point!

But, you see, pillows make me happy. Rocking horses and

sailboats and watering cans and baby carriages make me happy, too. Very, very happy.

Does that make me a bad person?

Anyway, I like my pillows more than I like some of our guests, so there.

A Nobel Effort, Per Se

RECENTLY TWO DEAR FRIENDS OF MINE, SARA O'MEARA AND Yvonne Fedderson of Childhelp, were honored together by Clarins Inc. with the Most Dynamic Woman Award. Nobody deserves this honor more. They've been nominated the past three years for the Nobel Peace Prize for all the amazing work they've done in the area of the prevention of child abuse.

And they would have won, except global warming was sexier, and Al Gore flat-out robbed them. Sorry. But I love these women so much, and they've dedicated the last *fifty* years of their lives to helping the smallest, most vulnerable victims of child abuse, which is our NATIONAL SHAME.

Anyway, after a lovely awards presentation, the CEO of Clarins, Monsieur Christian Courtin-Clarins; his daughter; past recipients; and Sara and Yvonne and I headed off for a celebratory dinner at Per Se, a restaurant in the Time Warner Center.

Did I neglect to say that Per Se is one of the most expensive restaurants in all of New York City? Sorry, but that's an important point to this story.

Because this is the kind of restaurant that serves about twenty courses in the span of, oh, about three hours.

Now, I don't know anybody who needs to eat that much for that long, but nobody cares what I think. It's impossible to get a table at Per Se for months in advance, so call me stupid. Recession? *Resmeshion.*

Just the amount of dinnerware and utensils used in the course of one meal is enough to keep a generator going for two days. Seriously, whoever does the dishes at Per Se is deserving of an award for Per-Se-Verance.

But what's fun is watching the faces of the diners there for the first time. They have been told in advance only that they are in for the gastronomic experience of a lifetime. And then, amid much fanfare, the first course is served. It's a bean. That's right. It's a bean in a big bowl. This would not normally go over well at, say, Outback Steakhouse in Staten Island.

But here, in the heart of Manhattan—"Oooh! A *bean*!"

Having dined here before, I am enjoying watching the reaction to the various courses as they arrive.

"Wow! A leaf!"

"Stop it! A lentil!"

"Get out of here! A radish with a dollop of crème fraîche!"

At this point I am only grateful that they serve far more wine than they do food.

I fell in love with Monsieur Clarins when he took a very long look at something that was put in front of him and then asked in a very French accent, "What the hell is this?"

"Oh," the waiter answered solemnly, "parsley."

"Oooh . . ."

Next time they're in town, I'm taking the whole crowd to Neary's Pub at Fifty-seventh Street and First Avenue for the greatest lamb chops or corned beef and cabbage they've ever had.

At about one hundredth the price.

P.S. Per Se *is* the gastronomic experience of a lifetime, because once the check arrives, you want to take a sharp utensil from in front of you and thrust it into your heart, thus ending your so-called life.

Wild Wednesday Women
or
TTELLIW

MOST PEOPLE LIKE FRIDAYS A LOT. IT'S THE ONLY DAY OF THE WEEK that's got it's own acronym: TGIF. It even has its own restaurant chain. My friend Dee says there's a really dirty acronym for Thursday, but I don't think it's caught on yet.

Me? I'm a Wednesday kind of woman: TTELLIW, Thank the Ever Lovin' Lord It's Wednesday. That's my motto, baby, and I'll tell you why. Because Wednesday is the weekday when the hardest working people in the world—Broadway performers—work twice as hard.

Only Times Square hookers do more shows in a day, but last I heard, it's mostly gymnastics. They're known for their moves, but not the Bob Fosse kind. They're known for hitting some high notes, but they can't hold one as long as Patti LuPone does in *Gypsy*.

So ever since I joined the *Today* show, Hoda and I have

made a date to have lunch at a great New York restaurant and then see whatever matinee is wowing 'em on Broadway. Thank goodness there's always a two P.M. curtain, or we'd both be three-hundred-pound alcoholics.

Christine, my beautiful assistant (she types this stuff, so I had to say that), usually goes with us. So does Sunny Luciani, a woman who started out as a fan of *Live* and quickly became a stalker, and within a very short time became a very good girl-friend. I love Sunny. Why? Because she's nuts. She's certifiably fun/funny/nuts the way I like my lunch partners to be. Well, that trip in from Connecticut must be pretty arduous for her, because Sunny is usually on her second glass of chardonnay by the time Christine and Hoda and I get to the restaurant. Which means that Sunny is already very, very happy when we arrive.

And when Sunny's happy, the whole world is happy, let me tell you. The fact that she usually falls asleep during the first act doesn't bother us a bit. We've been known to take a few winks, too, truth be told.

Sometimes Sunny doesn't like the show. It's rare, because Sunny as I mentioned is a very happy woman even when a show stinks. But when she loves one? Well, Sunny has seen *Jersey Boys* twenty-three times, so that tells you everything.

But once in a while she'll give us the old intermission "Can you believe this crap? I'm out of here" look and make her way home to Connecticut. I mean, I assume she makes it home, be-cause she's always there waiting for us at some new restaurant around noon the following Wednesday. So I warned Hoda that Sunny was a character before they met for the first time. Now every week she just asks, "Where are we meeting Sunny?"

One of my great joys has been watching Hoda discover the

extraordinary world of theater. I mean, this is a woman who has spent a great deal of time in prison.

It's true. Every time I'm off to a recording session or hurrying home to Frank and the kids, or shopping, or the dentist, or wherever, Hoda is invariably off to Rikers Island to interview some psycho who's just blown away her husband. This hard news coverage has been the stuff of her career for more than fifteen years. So I loved watching her reaction when we first went to see *Gypsy, South Pacific, A Chorus Line,* and *Grease.* She just *inhaled* it. She couldn't imagine how she had been so close to this magical world for so long without ever realizing what she was missing.

Finally, this midlife motley crew says goodbye on Wednesday evenings, and then on Thursdays, Hoda and I talk on *Today* about the show we saw. It's been a win-win situation for Broadway and for our television audience.

The hard part is discussing a show we didn't particularly like. Especially for me because I know all too well how hard everyone has worked and how many dreams are wrapped up in a production, not to mention how many jobs are at stake. And, worse, how many of those jobs are filled by really good friends of mine.

So, I guess you can tell when I don't particularly like a show by how little I say about it. I just can't lie. But I've found you can always find something good about pretty much anything. And that's true about life in general, don't you think?

So I guess I'm a lousy critic. There's already enough meanness in the world, so why add to it? But kindness and fairness? They're both in short supply.

I truly believe that as long as there are people in this world like Sunny Luciani, we'll be just fine, even when it isn't Wednesday.

Now my new goal in life is to write a Broadway musical that Sunny loves even more than *Jersey Boys*.

'Cause with friends like that . . . it'll run forever.

That Bella Fella

IN NOVEMBER 2007 I GOT A FATEFUL PHONE CALL FROM MY GOOD friend Emilie. She is one of those dear souls who love to put people together and make things happen. She and her husband, Craig, and their four kids travel all over the world on their boat, *Steadfast,* and are constantly impacting people's lives in wonderfully special ways.

So when Emilie calls, I know something's up.

"Kath," she began, "we're having a screening of this awesome new movie called *Bella.* Have you heard of it?"

"Yeah." I remembered. "I've been seeing some ads for it on TV. You mean the guy with the long beard?"

"Uh-huh," she said, and she went on to invite us to Florida, where she was going to be screening the film.

Unfortunately, I was recuperating from foot surgery and wasn't up for walking, much less flying.

"Then here's the number of the producer, Sean Wolfington," she insisted. "Call him and he'll come to your house with Eduardo, the star, and you can have a screening of your own."

There's something about Emilie that makes you do exactly what Emilie tells you to do. Just ask her husband.

So I called Sean on a Friday, and by Monday he and Eduardo Verástegui were at our house in Connecticut with about twenty invited guests on their way over.

Now, Emilie had told me that *Bella* was amazing. But she neglected to warn me that Eduardo is THE MOST BEAUTI-FUL MAN ON THE PLANET. He is called the Mexican Brad Pitt, but that is a compliment to Brad Pitt, believe me.

Frank had welcomed them and sent them to our guest suite to get ready while I was over in the other side of the house preparing for the party. I hobbled up the stairs in those unbelievably ugly post-surgery black booties they make you wear and knocked on the door to greet them. Sean opened the door, and I was surprised by how young, tall, and handsome he was. He could have been the star of the movie himself.

And then Eduardo came out, and I thought I would faint. I am not kidding you. I have met many gorgeous, GORGEOUS people in my life but for sheer physical perfection? Eduardo takes the prize.

Then he spoke with that Latin accent, and I pretty much had to pack it in.

Now, most of the guests that were invited to the screening are very sophisticated "seen it all, done it all" kind of people.

Well, they'd never seen Eduardo, let me tell ya.

Every last woman made pretty much a complete fool of herself. The men weren't much better.

Eduardo handled all the adoration with extraordinary

graciousness. I guess he's been insanely gorgeous since birth and he's gotten used to it.

Even Frank, who is no slouch in the looks department, said "He's too pretty to be a boy." You gotta love Frank.

Well, the evening was a smash, everybody loved the film, and it was hard to get those women out of my house.

But by then it had been decided that Eduardo would stay on a few days so I could help get some publicity for *Bella* through my media contacts.

I had more fun standing at my front door as our guests left, taunting them with "Eduardo's sleeping at *my* house! Na, na, na, na, na, na," like some stupid little kid.

He ended up staying for several days, and I arranged a couple of interviews for him. We didn't have an extra alarm clock so I had to go and *wake him up* every morning. I literally had to pray for strength, climbing those stairs to heaven.

But it turns out that, amazingly, once you get to know Eduardo, it's impossible to lust after him. Because he is so spiritual—so downright "unearthly" that it's almost like lusting after an angel. He even wears Angel cologne.

In a nutshell, here's his story: Born in a small Mexican town. Raised by loving Catholic parents. He joins a boy band when he's eighteen called Kairo and becomes an instant sensation. Girls mob him. He goes on to star in those telenovelas on Mexican TV and becomes an even bigger star. Now it's women who mob him. He leads the life of a rock star with all the accompanying excesses. He moves to Hollywood to become a movie star. He finally falls on his knees one day in repentance before God and makes a promise that he will never again use his talents in any way that offends his family, his God, or his race.

Now, this really limits one's show business opportunities.

Can you imagine going to your agent and telling him, "Look, I really want to work, but I won't do nudity or love scenes. I won't play a drug dealer or a Latin lothario. I won't cuss and I won't embarrass my mother in any way." Good luck, buddy.

When I met Eduardo, he had already been celibate for five years. Now it's been six. He's waiting for the woman he will marry.

Obviously, he's a pretty rare species.

But he practices what he preaches. He goes to Mass every day wherever he is. He even dragged me to Saint Patrick's Cathedral one day before lunch. It was beautiful, but maybe Eduardo had something to do with that.

I'm painfully aware that I could be Eduardo's *mother,* but when the inevitable tabloid headlines emerged, I've got to admit I got a kick out of them.

"Kathie Lee and Her Hot Young Latin Lover."

I mean, nobody believes these things, right?

Right.

P.S. When I first started on the *Today* show, we did the program outside in Rockefeller Plaza. A month later, when Eduardo was our guest, we made so much noise out on that Plaza that the fourth hour of the show was banned from broadcasting outside forever and into perpetuity and infinity and beyond. In other words, "Fuhgidaboutit." We call it the Eduardo Effect.

P.P.S. The Eduardo Effect continued. I was so inspired by the film that I wrote the lyrics to a song called "Everyone Has a Story." David Friedman added a poignant melody, and it became the title song for our *Today* show series by the same name.

One of the most thrilling experiences of my creative life has been taking so-called ordinary people's lives and writing a song with David for them.

Each time the person sat on that *Today* show couch and one of Broadway's extraordinary performers sang them their song, I had to pinch myself.

And my mind always returned to all the things Sitting Shiva told me so many years before: "Find something you love to do . . . learn to make your own music . . . give until it hurts." And so much more.

EVERYONE HAS A STORY

Everyone has a story
Different as night and day
And everyone has their own journey
Some follow their path, some wander away

But everyone has a moment
That changes their life, and then
It's suddenly clear in that moment
That nothing will ever be the same again

Careful the plans we make
Careful the roads we take
Careful the hearts we break
Along the way

Careful the things embraced
Careful the time we waste
Careful the dreams we taste
And toss away

Everyone has a purpose
Different as day and night

And everyone finds their own answer
Some blinded by fear, some guided by light

Yes, everyone has a story
A beginning, a middle, and end
But if there's a God in the heavens above
And if there's such a thing as a thing called love
Then there must be a way for anyone's heart to mend

Careful the chance we take
Careful the choice we make
Careful, for heaven's sake
The road we take . . .
Everyone has a story

'Nuff Said

A FEW YEARS BACK FRANK AND I WERE ASKED TO PRESENT AN award at the FiFi's—the international fragrance award in New York City. I have no idea why we said yes—oh, yeah, I had a new fragrance out—but anyway, we showed up for the big red carpet lineup beforehand with mixed emotions, because these types of events are always a zoo.

There was a massive sea of paparazzi because Sharon Stone was expected and so was Dame Elizabeth Taylor, who rarely attended such events anymore.

I don't know how it happened, but Frank and I were sent out for pictures along with the old White Diamond herself, Elizabeth Taylor, in all her splendor—just the three of us.

It was a "Waldo" moment that went on and on and on because the press just couldn't get enough of La Liz.

Finally I felt some small talk was in order, so I casually remarked, "You know, my husband hates these things as much as you do."

Well, she fixed those violet eyes on me in a flash and said without an ounce of humor, "I seriously doubt that."

So, no more needed to be said, because what more was there to say?

P.S. Sharon Stone was fun at dinner. At least Frank thought so.

Horsing Around

WELL, I'VE JUST SEEN HARRY POTTER'S MAGIC WAND. UP CLOSE and personal. In the flesh, on a stage on Forty-fourth Street, from four rows back.

Daniel Radcliffe, the young actor made famous by his portrayal of the wizard Harry Potter in the series of films, is currently starring on Broadway in a revival of *Equus,* a searing drama of psychological, sexual teenage angst that asks the question: "Who's really crazy?"

The answer to that is probably the schmucks paying four hundred dollars a ticket to see Harry buck naked in a state of ecstasy astride a sort of iron-meshed horse-man. Not that Daniel isn't good in it; in fact, he's excellent. But I doubt the show is SRO (standing room only) because people are suddenly interested in the complexities of mental illness.

But here's the fun part. Right after the second act started, my friend Sunny's cell phone went off just as the psychiatrist treating Harry is starting to lose it big-time himself. I was sitting to Sunny's right and immediately acted like I had no idea who she was and "why do they allow people like that into the theater in the first place?"

Sunny kept trying to turn it off, but the harder she tried the louder it got. It was a brand-new iPhone she obviously had not yet mastered. And of course it was playing some stupid song from *Jersey Boys* or something.

Well, Sunny high-tailed it up the aisle with the offending device clutched tightly to her flop bags as the audience hissed their disgust.

Finally, safe in the lobby, she begged an usher to hold the phone for her until after the show.

"Is he naked yet?" she kept asking the unfortunate guy. "Have I missed it?"

The usher calmly took her phone and answered, "No, lady, you've still got a couple of minutes."

Sunny then nonchalantly walked back down the aisle, took her seat, and put on her glasses.

Waiting for the magic.

Let's put it this way: She says the wand was worth the wait.

P.S. Just as this manuscript went to print, Sunny checked herself into an alcohol treatment facility. I am so proud of her and the courage it takes to recognize and deal with what had become a problem in her life.

Instinkt

People often ask me if I ever regret something I say or do on the air.

Truthfully, the answer is yes I do, pretty much every day. But the reason I can live guilt-free is that I know my own heart and it is never my intention to be hurtful to anyone in any way at any time.

So with that disclaimer out of the way, comedy can be DANGEROUS. It's a high-wire act with no net, and you should never attempt it if you're faint of heart or weak of stomach or shy of nature. And once you're up there, there's no turning back.

Last summer I dodged a major bullet, and I felt terrible about it at the time, but it illustrates my point exactly. We have a wonderful segment on Fridays called Plaza Ambush Makeovers. Basically our two experts, Jill Martin and Louis

Licari, choose two people from the audience gathered out on the plaza and spend the next couple of hours totally making them over. Then they reveal the results during our ten A.M. hour, and everybody goes home happy.

It's a very popular segment, and it's often very moving, too. Many of the people chosen have recently been through traumatic experiences and need a little life-lift.

One morning in July I arrived early at the studio with wet hair and dark sunglasses. It was a typical morning until suddenly I noticed Jill and a *Today* show crew interviewing a woman. I was quite a distance from them so I couldn't hear what was going on, but I could tell I was directly in the line of camera view.

I had two choices. I could try to run by and hide my identity or I could go the old "let 'er rip" way and have a little fun.

Well, "instinct" took over and I began mugging for the camera as if I were channeling Jerry Lewis. The camera moved away, so I moved with it and started to "walk like an Egyptian."

Once again the camera moved away, so, what the hell, I did, too, and did a very good impression of Robin Williams from *Mork & Mindy*. I basically did every stupid thing I could do without dropping my pants and mooning the camera.

And then, satisfied that it had indeed been hysterical, I continued on my way into the studio.

About halfway there my heart stopped. I just suddenly thought, "Oh, my God! What if they had been talking about something serious?"

So I went to warn Brian, our producer, to check the tape. He turned white.

"Kathie," he said, trying to stay calm, "that lady's mother died of a brain tumor."

"Oh, no!" I said.

"And the next week her father died of another brain tumor!"

"OH MY GOD!"

"And she had just buried them both."

"SH@#?!!ZUKI!!"

"And then . . ."

"STOP! STOP!" I screamed. "Don't tell me more. You've got to get that tape before it airs!"

Luckily we were able to ward off a terribly upsetting incident.

But what if I hadn't followed my other instinct—the one that warned that it might be serious?

Well, I shudder to think of the pain it could have caused that lady and whoever's left in her family.

See? Comedy is dangerous.

Z-100

Way, way back in time—in fact, B.F.; 1985, before Frank—
I had a small house in the Hamptons that a lovely Chinese couple used to care for when I was working in New York.

Zhi and Liann Lin had been in America with their small
son, Daniel, for several years, hoping to become nationalized
citizens.

One day Zhi informed me that they could no longer continue working for me because they needed to move to Flushing, New York, so that Daniel could attend a special school for
gifted children.

This happened to coincide with my own decision to move
to Connecticut full-time and commute to work in the city.

I needed a driver, so I offered the new position to Zhi, who
promptly accepted.

Zhi has now been with me for twenty-four years. He has

driven me everywhere you can possibly imagine, and I, in turn, have driven him crazy, which you can probably imagine very easily.

But you'd never know it to look at Zhi. He has one answer for anything I ask of him: "No problem."

Eventually Daniel went on to get his law degree from Columbia University. The kid's a genius.

"Zhi," I said to him, "please don't be offended, but when I was growing up, all the Asian kids were so much smarter than anybody else."

"Not smarter," Zhi responded immediately. "Work harder."

For years Zhi quietly and dependably carted me to studios, airports, restaurants, department stores, doctors' appointments—you name it. He was always there, always smiling, and never complaining.

Until one day in 1991 when I asked him to take me some place the next day.

"No tomorrow," he suddenly said—two words I had never heard him utter.

"Zhi," I told him, "that's fine, but do you mind my asking why not?"

"Tomorrow get citizenship," he answered simply.

I wanted to cry I was so proud for him, but I wouldn't dare embarrass him.

It was around this time, just when I started to think that Zhi was truly becoming Americanized, that I offered him a raise. Zhi immediately responded, "No, you pay me too much already."

It's a good thing Zhi hasn't met my truly patriotic agent. . . .

Gone but Not Forgotten

FOR ME THE HARDEST PART OF GETTING OLDER IS NOT THE FEAR OF my own death but the heartbreak of the deaths of people I love. Like my daddy.

It used to be that Frank and I went to a lot of christenings, bar mitzvahs, and weddings.

Now we go to an awful lot of funerals.

I recently looked at a mural of pictures taken on our wedding day, October 18, 1986. It was a glorious Indian summer day in Bridgehampton, New York, at the beachside home of our dear friends Ron and Isobel Konecky.

About seventy people attended, and now more than half of them are gone.

Most of them had been Frank's friends, who of course were around Frank's age at the time. People like Roone Arledge and Pete Rozelle.

But others, like my precious friend Claudia Cohen, were much younger.

Claudia tragically died of ovarian cancer in the summer of 2007. She left behind a beautiful daughter, Samantha, who was born three months after Cody and was the absolute joy of Claudia's life, and Claudia left more grieving friends than you can count.

Then there's my sweet friend Nancy LaMott, who died at the age of forty-three in 1995 of uterine cancer.

Nobody had more talent than Nancy. She was the finest interpreter of the Great American Songbook of this generation, and to this day I can't hear her voice without crying.

We became friends when my pal David Friedman sent me a demo of eight songs to consider recording for an upcoming album. Every one of the songs was terrific, but what really made an impression on me was the vocalist on the tape. David informed me that it was a well-known cabaret singer from Midland, Michigan, named Nancy LaMott.

He also told me that she needed to have a surgery performed that my sister had had many years before, known as an ileostomy.

This is a nasty procedure that basically redirects a person's digestive tract from the anus to an opening in the abdomen, where it drains into a bag taped onto the side of the body.

Michie had it done thirty-one years ago, and it saved her life. But it was only one of Nancy's many physical problems. I was able to connect Nancy with Michie, and it comforted Nancy a great deal to discuss it with someone who had actually been through it.

Eventually we all fell in love with Nancy and her talent. You couldn't separate one from the other.

I tried to champion her every chance I could on *Live* and everywhere else.

In the year before she died she performed two times at the White House, on *Live,* and on *Good Morning America.* She was on the verge of true stardom when she ignored a doctor's cancer diagnosis and put off surgery until a new album was completed.

It was a fatal choice.

The last few months of her life were spent undergoing chemo and radiation that wreaked havoc with her already devastated body, battling cancer that had spread to her liver.

On weekends Zhi would drive her to our house in Connecticut, and Frank would cook for her and I'd pray with her and we'd talk about music and men and life and the afterlife for hours and hours.

Finally in December I held up her Christmas album, *Just in Time for Christmas,* on *Live* and said, "If you get the people you love nothing else this Christmas, get them this album."

After the show I walked into my dressing room, and my assistant, Taryn, ashen-faced, said, "Kathie, you've got to get to the hospital. Nancy's in ICU."

Ten minutes later I stumbled through the intensive care wing at Roosevelt Hospital and completely walked by Nancy's bed. She was that unrecognizable. She had been bald for several months, but now her cheekbones protruded from her face, her eyes were hollowed, and her nostrils were stuffed with blood-soaked cotton.

She was literally bleeding to death.

I couldn't let her see the shock I was feeling, so I said, "Oh, nice. I'm on TV bustin' my butt trying to sell your album, and you're here lying on your ass."

Nancy started giggling. I noticed her toes exposed at the bottom of her sheet, and I did something I had never done before. I started to kiss her toes. I have no idea why. But those toes looked so tender and vulnerable and so unbelievably sad that I had to.

"It's a good thing you're so cute," I told her. "Look at these toes! They're beautiful."

Then I kissed her all the way up her body until my tear-drenched face reached her beautiful bald head.

Laughing and crying, we held each other, and I rocked her like you rock a sick, dying child, because she was.

"Oh, Nance," I finally told her, "God needs a soloist in His choir."

She nodded, and I knew she understood from all our talks by the fireside that long and painful fall.

And then I looked at her for the last time and whispered into her tiny, sweet ear, "When I get to heaven, will you teach me to sing?"

The Letter *I*

PEOPLE LOOKING FOR A DETAILED EXPOSÉ ON WHAT FRANK AND I
went through in our marriage back in the 1990s will be disappointed not to find it in this book.

I have said everything I needed to say in interviews and ar-
ticles over the years since, and so has Frank.

There truly comes a time when enough is enough and any
more does nothing but cause more harm and more pain, as if
picking a scab over and over again, making it impossible to finally heal.

But I do think that the *concept* of forgiveness is one that
can never be brought up enough.

Because I believe that I can't ask for mercy unless I'm willing to also offer mercy. And boy, do I need mercy.

There is a perception that I'll talk about anything, share
anything, regardless of how silly or sacred.

Frank and I have no trouble remembering each others' birthdays. We were both born August 16—*many* years apart.

But the truth is, that's not true at all.

I have secrets. Lots of secrets. About myself and about others, and they will go to a hopefully very distant grave with me. Why? Because some things are absolutely nobody else's business, that's why.

I understand the "public's right to know" when it comes to matters of national interest and security. But the public's right to know every aspect of anyone's personal life? Absolutely not. When it comes to our personal lives, every human being should have the right to reveal what they want and withhold what they choose for their own personal reasons.

It's guaranteed under the Constitution as defined by "the pursuit of happiness." Or at least it's supposed to be.

But I'm also aware that we can learn a great deal from

other people's mistakes, and I feel a responsibility to share whatever has been helpful in my own life, in the hopes that it will be helpful in someone else's.

So, in that spirit, I'm comfortable in saying that I would be dead without forgiveness. Or somebody else would. Or I'd be in prison, or in an asylum or in a rehab center. But I definitely would not be a (relatively) mentally healthy, happy, functioning, grateful human being.

Because withholding forgiveness ultimately destroys the person unwilling to forgive. It's a malignancy of the soul that decays you from within, embitters and poisons you in pathetic self-centeredness and pride. It saps all joy from your life and leaves you in an emotional fetal position unable to function, much less thrive.

Basically, it kills you from the inside out. An emotional ebola.

We all make mistakes. We all hurt ourselves and others. Sometimes we mean to, and sometimes we're just weak and crap happens. I tell the kids all the time, "You're one decision away from disaster," because it's true. For all of us.

And yet I remember Sitting Shiva wisely telling me many years ago, "I love you too much to deny you the privilege of making mistakes." I thought he was crazy at the time, but now I think he was a genius.

So I'm careful to also tell the kids, "Even if you make a bad decision and disaster happens, nothing can change my love for you." We can hate their choice and still love the person who made it.

It's okay to be angry when it happens. It's natural. But we can't *stay* angry.

We can and should mourn what is lost because of a betrayal.

But we can't stay in mourning forever.
We can be bitter or we can be better.
It's all in the letter *I*. And it's all up to us.
I choose love so *I* can have life.
And life abundant.

No Country for Old Women

Your DNA determines your children's physical attributes, but it also goes down deeper than bone marrow to their very dreams and aspirations.

Cassidy has known that she wants to be an actress for as long as she can remember being asked that immortal question "What do you want to be when you grow up?"

Frank and I don't often agree about her chosen path, and it creates not a little bit of tension in our family dynamic because, although we share the same concerns regarding our kids' futures, we just disagree on how to deal with them. We'll get through it—it's hardly the toughest thing we'll face together—but it makes for some lively conversations, let me tell ya.

Forget being a librarian, now Frank would prefer that Cassidy become a nun. I, however, think we should do every-

thing for Cass that we did for Cody, and that means supporting and encouraging her interest as much as we can. No double standards allowed.

Recently Cass got a call to audition in Los Angeles for a
guest-starring role in a cute Disney TV series called *Wizards of
Wavery Place*. A week later she got a callback and excitedly
taped her second audition via the Internet.

Things have changed dramatically since my first years in
the business, and I watched with great admiration as she went
about setting up her computer, checking the lighting, touching
up her minimal hair and makeup, and then performing her
lines, downloading the video, and emailing it to the producers
three thousand miles away. All in about ten minutes.

She felt great about the audition, and she had reason to.
We had worked on it. She and her acting coach had worked on
it, and the final product was excellent.

But I continue to remind her that she has picked an excru-
ciatingly difficult career. You want rejection? You'll get it up
to your eyeballs. You want criticism? You won't have to wait
long. You want heartache? You'll get it every time the choice
comes down to you and somebody else and that somebody else
gets the job.

In regard to Cassidy, I have been brutal in telling the truth
about this industry that I love and that has been awfully good
to me. Not sugarcoating the downside, which includes rejection, scrutiny, and a constant sense of judgment from both the
industry and the public. Frank has told Cody the brutal truth
about football, both the highs and the lows. I think that's just
part of what we parents are supposed to do.

So now she is learning firsthand the realities of show business. It has been one week since she sent in her second audi-

tion, and the episode is scheduled to begin taping in L.A. to-morrow.

Obviously she didn't get the role. But I couldn't let her sit next to the telephone all week long waiting to hear the news, while life went on all around her. She can try to make a living in this business, but she should never let it become her life. The same thing is true about a man.

"Don't sit by the phone and wait for a man *or* a job," I keep telling her.

"Go out and make the best of each moment you're given, and never give *anyone* or *anything* more power over you than you have over yourself."

I have so many friends who have fallen into this trap, and I admit that I have been guilty of it at times in my own life. But I don't think we should spend our lives waiting *for* a man and then spend the rest of it waiting *on* him.

Loving someone does not mean losing the essence of our-selves to that person. I want my children to be happy and healthy like any mother does. But I think it's so much more important what they *are* than what they *do*.

I saw a quote the other day from Joanie's favorite philoso-pher, Anon, that says it all: "Go out into the world and do well; but more importantly—go out into the world and do good."

P.S. At this moment Cass has come *thisclose* to two major film deals and is being considered for various other television proj-ects. Obviously our lives could change at any moment with one phone call. But she's not waiting for it.

She just took up tap dancing.

Atta girl.

The Doctor Is in but She's a Little Late

IN MAY OF 1997, I FINALLY GRADUATED FROM COLLEGE. WELL, sort of.

Marymount University gave me an honorary doctorate of humane letters for all my efforts to eradicate labor abuse in the world.

It was a tremendous honor, and I have to admit—call me human, but it felt damn good to be praised instead of crucified for a change.

As I gave the commencement address and looked out at all the eager, excited faces of the graduates, it was hard to hold back all the emotions I was feeling.

I wanted to warn them. I wanted to hold them close and keep them from making mistakes. I wanted to help them understand how bad life can get and how hard it can be, but how much it's worth the struggle.

I wanted to tell them how incredibly special they are and how wondrous the future can be if they work hard and keep the faith that they know in their hearts is true.

Good for you, kids. Go, set the world on fire. Find something you love to do and then find a way to get paid for it. Soar. Make your parents proud and your Creator smile. Make no enemies and let your river flow until every single dream you ever dreamed has been set free. Let no obstacle deter you. Let no unkind word cause you to be unkind in return. Understand that every opportunity placed before you is a precious gift, not realized until you take it by the hand and share it with somebody else. Say "please" and "thank you" and "you're welcome" every time you should.

Say "I love you" only when you really mean it, and learn to say "I'm sorry" even when you don't.

Never take something from someone else that was never yours to begin with.

Respect those who have come before you and climbed mountains you have only read about.

Laugh every single chance you get, but only when the laughter is at no one's expense but your own.

Stop to taste every delicious bite and smell every delectable scent that comes with it.

Touch every heart that is hurting and ease every pain that you recognize on someone else's face as pain you have felt before.

Share every meager meal with someone who is hungry and share your tattered coat with someone who is cold, and you will never feel hungry or cold again.

Treasure each day for the gift that it is, and never watch a sunrise or a sunset without wonder and gratitude in your soul.

Walk at least one step in someone else's Manolo Blahnik's or flip-flops before you pass judgment on them. Then love them as if you are guilty of the very same thing, because chances are, you are.

Choose to forgive even when it breaks your heart, because it *will* break your heart if you don't.

Take your pulse and check your purpose every morning, and you'll sleep peacefully every night.

Learn something new every day of your life and then live truly and authentically with every ounce of your being, turning your daydreams into dream days while you still can.

Practice kindness as if the world depended on it. Because, ya know what?

It does.

Good Morning

I WOKE UP EARLIER THAN FRANK THIS MORNING, WHICH HARDLY ever happens. But we're here in Nantucket and I've got a lot on my mind. The sun is beginning to rise and I'm on my second cup of coffee. I've had my devotions and a little prayer time, and I feel very peaceful and content.

But now I'm thinking of my mom, waking up all alone in her apartment. It's been six years since Daddy died, and Mom says it's loneliest when she opens her eyes in the morning and Daddy's not beside her, and when she closes them again at night and he still isn't.

I've been a "football widow" at times just like most women, but I can't imagine what it must be like to be a real widow. I know Mom has peace that Daddy is in the arms of God, but I'm sure she'd rather have him back in hers.

So I say a little prayer that she will have a wonderful, blessed day, and I wait for my husband to come downstairs and share mine with me.

Each day is a gift. That's why it's called the present.

Unwrap it.

My favorite picture ever of my mom and dad, at Cassidy's third birthday party. They both look so happy and so alive.

Writer's Block

You know what's so weird? Somewhere along the line I somehow completely forgot that I wrote my first book when I was twenty. It was called *The Quiet Riot* and it chronicled my teen years and my first love and my spiritual awakening at the age of thirteen. It was published by Fleming H. Revell and went through three printings. It's embarrassing to read it today—it seems like a completely different person wrote it.

But how is it possible to *forget* something like that? I mean, why didn't I see the signs even then that I might be a writer?

Or when I wrote stupid songs about my dogs and kids. Why didn't I realize then that I might have the ability to write serious songs if I worked at it?

I mean, granted, "Chardonnay's a fur ball, a fur ball from hell / Chardonnay's a fur ball, but I think she's swell" is not exactly up there with "Somewhere" from *West Side Story*. But it's a *beginning,* and sometimes beginning something is the hardest part.

I think I have been such a huge fan of good writing for so long—I have so much respect for the people who really know their craft—that any effort that wasn't up to that standard wasn't worth the effort in the first place.

In other the words, if I couldn't be right up there with the best of the best, I was better off finding something else to try to excel at.

The trouble with this reasoning is that it's not reasonable.

We encourage our children to draw pictures. We don't expect them to be Picasso right off the bat.

We encourage them to take up a musical instrument, but we don't expect to hear anything but a lot of really horrific sounds for a very long time before anything anywhere near beautiful begins to emanate from little Tommy's tuba.

And when little Lily puts on her first tutu, we just ooh and aah over how adorable she is. We couldn't care less if she can't plié yet. In fact, at that point we don't care if she can walk. It's just so much fun to look at her.

"Get on with your point, Kathie Lee," I can hear you muttering. I'm trying, believe me. I'm just attempting to figure out where I went wrong so I can help you out of that midlife rut you may find yourself in.

You're welcome.

Anyway, the signs were there in my own life that deep down inside I had more gifts than I realized. And so do you. I think everyone does.

Reach back in your memory to when you were little. What did you love to do? What couldn't your mother drag you away from? What made you happy every time you did it? What did you dream about? Whatever it was, I truly think that that is what you were *meant* to do. Time and circumstances have a way of changing the course of our path, but that original path is still there. Hidden by cobwebs and weeds and a whole bunch of emotional garbage, probably, but nonetheless still there.

It's not too late to go looking for it. It might surprise you how close it is.

Check your closet.

If that old tutu or tuba is in there, chances are your dreams are, too.

What Do I Want?

DURING THE DARKEST DAYS OF MY LIFE WHEN I COULD BARELY hear my own heartbeat because of the raging storm around me, I sat down and tried to put on paper words that could express the longing of my battered soul.

Some twelve years later, they still do.

I WANT TO MATTER

I want to matter

To have meant something special to somebody else
To have made a small difference simply being myself
To believe this three-ring circus
Has fulfilled some earthly purpose

I want to matter, before I am gone
To have once been the shoulder that someone leaned on

To have been the safe harbor in someone's sad storm
To know someone was blessed
Because I was born

I want to matter
As much as I'm able
To be more than a faded face, framed on some table
For if I'm to be framed, I want it to be
In somebody's heart for eternity

Tho I'm fragile and foolish and flawed—I'm sincere
I want someone to fondly remember me here

More than being praised, more than being flattered
I need to know without a doubt that somehow I have
  mattered

And if I'm really honest
I would like to be the song
That someone will be singing
Long after I am gone

Acknowledgments

Even when you write a book by yourself, there are always many people that need to be acknowledged and thanked for all their invaluable assistance. It has been so much fun working with my agent, Mel Berger, at the William Morris Agency. He was the first to think this book could work, and he's crazy enough to think the next three will, too.

Many thanks to Pamela Cannon, my editor, who never once conveyed that she thought I was crazier than Mel. On the contrary, she laughed in all the appropriate places, made excellent suggestions about what to lengthen, shorten, clarify, or basically DUMP. Usually she was right, but not always, and we never came to blows.

Charles Bush took whimsical, flattering pictures of me for which I am more eternally grateful to him than anybody else. I have my priorities, after all.

As always, Christine Gardner made sense of my chicken scratch and kept up with my feverish pace. I truly have no idea how I could ever live without her, and I pray to God I never have to.

And finally I have to thank my extraordinary family, friends, and colleagues who have allowed me to share their funny, poignant, and inspiring stories.

They have made my life a life worth living.

And loving.

And laughing about.

About the Author

KATHIE LEE GIFFORD is best known for her fifteen-year role as co-host of the nationally syndicated television show *Live with Regis and Kathie Lee*. She recently returned to television as co-host of the fourth hour of NBC's *Today* show. She is the author of six books, including the bestselling memoir *I Can't Believe I Said That!*, and has recorded sixteen albums. She is currently writing and producing a number of stage musicals. She lives in Connecticut with her husband and children.